Ethical Dilemmas
in
Jewish Communal Service

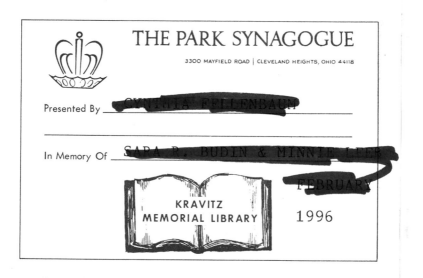

Ethical Dilemmas
in
Jewish Communal Service

by

Norman Linzer

KTAV Publishing House, Inc.

Association of Jewish Family & Children's Agencies

Jewish Communal Service Association

Library of Congress Cataloging-in-Publication Data

Linzer, Norman.
    Ethical dilemmas in Jewish communal service / by Norman Linzer.
        p.   cm.
    Includes bibliographical references and index.
    ISBN 0-88125-516-5 $39.50   0-88125-532-7 $19.95
    1. Jews--United States--Charities--Moral and ethical aspects.
    2. Social work--United States--Moral and ethical aspects. 3. Social
    workers--Professional ethics--United States. I. Title.
    HV3191.L56 1995
    361.7'5'088296--dc20   95-35866
                                                                        CIP

Manufactured in the United States of America

Dedicated to my wonderful family

Diane

Moshe and Rebecca
Aderet and Ronit

Dov and Debbie
Shoshana

Menachem

Michal

Contents

Acknowledgments

Ten chapters were written expressly for this book, two of which were adapted from presentations at professional meetings. Six chapters were published previously in various journals and modified for this book.

"Professional Ethics and Jewish Ethics" is adapted from presentations at a Board of Directors Institute, Jewish Family Services, Baltimore, Md., on June 13, 1991, and a staff training seminar, "Ethics and Halakhah," Ohel Children's Home and Family Services, Brooklyn, N.Y., Nov. 19, 1992.

"The Role of Values in Determining Agency Policy" was originally presented as a staff seminar, Jewish Family Services, Baltimore, Md., and published in *Families in Society* 73, no. 9 (November 1992), by Families International, Inc.

"Value Conflicts in Nursing Home Placement" was originally presented as a staff seminar, Jewish Family Services, Baltimore, Md., and published as "Ethical Decision-making: Implications for Practice," *Journal of Jewish Communal Service* 65, no. 3 (Spring 1989).

"Ethical Considerations in Serving Intermarried Couples" is a composite of two articles published in the *Journal of Jewish Communal Service* as "Ethical Considerations of Serving Intermarried Couples," 69, no. 1 (Fall 1992); and "Resolving Ethical Dilemmas in Jewish Communal Service," 63, no. 2 (Winter 1986).

"The Ethics of Circumventing the Waiting List" was published in the *Journal of Jewish Communal Service* 68, no. 2 (Winter 1991–92), and presented at a staff seminar, Social Service Department, Hillside Hospital, New Hyde Park, N.Y., on Oct. 25, 1993.

"Talmudic and Ethical Approaches to Resettlement of Jews

from the Former Soviet Union" was published in the *Journal of Jewish Communal Service* 67, no. 2 (Winter 1990), and presented at a Board of Directors seminar of New York Association of New Americans, April 18, 1990.

"Ethical Dilemmas in the Jewish Community Center" has been updated from its publication in the *Journal of Jewish Communal Service* 64, no. 2 (Winter 1987).

"Professional and Personal Priorities" was originally presented at a staff institute, Jewish Federation of Metrowest, April 2–3, 1992.

This project would not have come to fruition without the intellectual and critical support of an erudite group of professional colleagues in Jewish communal service. They read the manuscript carefully and suggested important changes in content and style that reflect the diversity of their ideologies, experience, and positions. In critiquing, updating the cases, and reviewing the text, they sharpened and attuned the approaches to diverse target audiences.

I am deeply grateful to the late David Dubin, executive director, Jewish Community Center of Tenafly, N.J.; Bert J. Goldberg, executive vice-president, Association of Jewish Family and Children's Agencies; Mark Handelman, executive director, New York Association for New Americans; Joseph Harris, consultant, Jewish Community Centers Association; William Kahn, former executive vice-president, St. Louis and New York Jewish Federations; Chaim Lauer, executive director, Board of Jewish Education of Greater Washington, Rockville, Md.; David Mann, executive vice-president, Board of Jewish Education of Greater New York; Dr. Bernard Reisman, director, Hornstein Program of Jewish Communal Service, Brandeis University, Waltham, Mass.; Dr. Jeffrey Solomon, chief operating officer, UJA-Federation of New York; and Dr. Lucy Steinitz, executive director, Jewish Family Services, Baltimore, Md.

Special mention must be made of my friend, colleague, and collaborator, Dr. Rivka Danzig, who worked with me in formulating the conception and structure of the book and the interview schedule.

I am indebted to the people who participated in the interviews and the agency executives who arranged them. Their cooperation and sharing of their ethical concerns inspired me.

Dr. Sheldon Gelman, dean of the Wurzweiler School of Social Work, made available the school's support system. In particular, Sylvia Baldwin's typing and organization of the materials were exemplary.

For all the hours and days spent at the computer and not being available for my family, I thank Diane, my wife, who has continuously supported my literary and professional endeavors with her patience and sage counsel.

Norman Linzer, Ph.D.
Samuel J. and Jean Sable Professor of Jewish Family Social Work
Wurzweiler School of Social Work
Yeshiva University

New York
June, 1995

Introduction

Ethics is in the air. Hardly a day goes by without a news story detailing breaches of ethical conduct in government, business, education, or the professions. We have become inured to the pervasiveness of the violators of the public trust and private interests. We shrug our shoulders and go on with our daily lives.

Daily life has become very complex. It is buffeted by changing values, pluralization of choices, threats to the moral authority of institutions, and the culture of narcissism. Traditional values are challenged, more life-style options are available, and we are no longer sure about what is right or wrong.

The Jewish community has not been immune to these societal trends. Jews have traversed the stages of acculturation and structural assimilation, and have entered the stage of marital assimilation (Gordon 1964). The rising rates of intermarriage, divorce, singlehood, single-parent families, later marriages, and low fertility point to the erosion of traditional Jewish values and the ascendance of contemporary secular values. Confirmed by the National Jewish Population Survey (Council of Jewish Federations 1991), these trends have aroused deep anxiety among Jewish communal leaders concerning the future of Jewish life in North America. Federations, bureaus of Jewish education, Jewish community centers, Jewish family services, and synagogues have expressed their determination to strengthen Jewish identity and continuity. The problem looms large because Jewish values and traditions are losing the competition with other value systems.

There are a number of value systems operating in Jewish communal services. They include Western cultural values, Jewish values (sometimes subdivided by the branch of Judaism), professional values (social work, nursing, Jewish education, law, etc.), government, community, and agency values, and client values. Staff values may be at variance with the Jewish purposes of agencies. Staff may not be Jewish, may be intermarried, and may display life-styles inconsistent with Jewish tradition. On any given issue, there are bound to be value differences that are reflected in disagreements over policies and programs to serve the community. Given the democratic nature of Jewish communal institutions, these diverse voices demand expression before consensus is reached in the resolution of the conflict.

A dominant cultural value is the development of the self as the raison d'etre of human existence. Self-gratification, self-determination, and self-actualization constitute an ideology that permeates individual consciousness and leads to actions that concentrate on the individual self rather than the group. This ethos is antithetical to a traditional Jewish ideology that emphasizes the needs and continuity of the community. In Jewish tradition there is an exquisite balance between the individual and the community, with some mitzvot (commandments) directed toward the individual, some to the community, and some to the individual in the community (Linzer 1978). Jews are expected to defer to communal needs and to contribute their resources and talents to the perpetuation of the community (Exodus 25:1–9). Community transcends the individual and provides belonging and stability.

In Jewish communal service, social workers, lawyers, psychologists, and business professionals subscribe to the principle of self-determination. Jewish educators and Jewish communal service workers may not give primacy to self-determination, but they know that clients seek self-expression. Clients' self-interest and thrust for self-gratification may clash with the communal interests of the staff, the agency, and the community.

By definition, value clashes lead to ethical conflicts. As a result, professionals in a variety of disciplines in Jewish communal agencies are confronted by ethical conflicts. Is it right to transfer funds allocated to Jewish education to serve immigrants from the former Soviet Union? Is it ethical to circumvent the waiting list at a home for the aged for a relative of a prominent lay leader? May a Jewish community center decline to serve homosexuals or the intermarried? How much leeway in sexual behavior should a Jewish family service give to the cognitively impaired residents in a group home? If federation cuts allocations to agencies, is it right to increase funding to one agency because a wealthy donor demands it? Can one ethically avoid firing a close friend when budget cuts demand it? These dilemmas represent a sample of those discussed in this book.

Professional practice is characterized by the demand for immediate response and action. Consciously or unconsciously, practitioners function with a degree of ethical coherence, although it usually remains unformulated. This book is an effort to put forth a more articulated statement of how practitioners actually deal with their ethical concerns, and the values, principles, and theories that could serve as a framework for resolving ethical dilemmas.

Ethical dilemmas are varied and complex, and do not readily lend themselves to easy resolution. In Jewish communal service, some dilemmas involve conflicts between an agency's Jewish purposes and values and its professional values and ethics. Sometimes the dilemma is "purely" a professional one unrelated to sectarian issues. Dilemmas include conflicting interests and loyalties, the needs of clients vs. the needs of the agency and community, the Jewish stake vs. the professional concern.

The aim of this book is to better understand the nature and resolution of ethical dilemmas in Jewish communal service. It is designed to assist social workers, practitioners of other professional disciplines, and students to identify, explain, and resolve ethical dilemmas in a rational and systematic manner. Though the analytical focus is on social work values and ethics, the model may be applied to other disciplines.

My interest in the process of resolving ethical dilemmas stems from my teaching in the Doctoral Program of the Wurzweiler School of Social Work. The purpose of the Doctoral Program is to develop scholarly practitioners who possess intellectual ability and an orderly way of thinking about, and influencing, social work practice, teaching, and social policy.

I have taught the Ideology course for the past thirteen years. Course content focuses on the values and ethics of social work and social welfare, and their impact on social work practice. Knowledge of values and ethics, as the major components of ideology, is viewed as an essential prerequisite for attaining practice skill. Students learn how to trace conflict situations in practice to value differences among the parties. Value conflicts are conceived as the source of ethical dilemmas.

The teaching process has also been a learning process regarding the complexities in understanding the nature of ideology and in determining the "right" decision in a conflict situation. Ethical ambiguities, however, instead of being an obstacle to continued exploration, have stimulated the pursuit of clarity. In the classroom, the more that is learned of the subject, the more challenging is the search for understanding.

Dr. Rivka Danzig, a former member of the Wurzweiler faculty, collaborated with me in formulating the design of this study. Her interest in this subject is of long standing. In her doctoral dissertation at Wurzweiler, she studied the moral dilemmas of Orthodox Jewish students as they grappled with conflicts between personal values and professional values. Currently she serves on the faculty of the University of Pennsylvania School of Social Work.

The subject of ethics touches me as a modern Orthodox Jew. Deeply committed to Jewish tradition and its viability in modern society, I believe that *Torah*—Jewish knowledge—can coexist with *mada*—secular knowledge. While integration or synthesis cannot always be attained, both systems of thought can enrich each other through their dialectical relationship.

The interface between Judaic and secular systems of thought has always intrigued me. It is the theme of the Jewish Social Philosophy course that I teach on the master's level, and has been the central theme of my professional writings. Of particular interest is the conflict between Judaic thought and professional values, and how they affect professional practice in Jewish agencies.

Conflicts in agencies may be attributed to different value orientations. Client values may differ with professional and agency values. The agency's Jewish component may be a source of conflict when clients, community, and staff disagree with their definition and implementation. The values of Judaism and the values of modern society do not always coincide and may lead to totally opposite positions on important issues. Conflict may also erupt when Judaic values are compared with professional values. The interface between Judaic values and professional values is a primary source of ethical dilemmas in Jewish communal service.

Deeply involved in the world of Jewish values, ethics, and tradition as a Jew and in the world of the service professions as a social worker, I have experienced conflicts between personal Jewish values and professional values. This book serves as the catalyst for grappling with these conflicts in a systematic manner in order to clarify them and chart paths to their resolution.

ASSUMPTIONS

Several assumptions provide the rationale for this book. They may be outlined as follows:

1. Professionals desire to act ethically out of the coincidence of personal convictions and professional imperatives. But when caught on the horns of an ethical dilemma and subject to pressures from several sides, they may not always do so.
2. There is confusion between ethical and practice dilemmas. What appears to be an ethical dilemma may in reality be a practice problem, and vice versa.
3. Professionals do not have the time to delineate and analyze ethical dilemmas because they are expected to act immediately.
4. Professionals do not possess the theoretical knowledge and analytical tools with which to resolve ethical dilemmas.
5. The mind-set of professionals is toward "doing" rather than thinking about the theoretical underpinnings of a problem.
6. The process of ethical decision making can be taught in a rational, systematic manner.

While the ultimate aim of this book is to provide practitioners with the tools for analyzing and resolving ethical dilemmas, particular decisions are not prescribed. Practitioners are not told what to do. The conceptual bases of the options prepare practitioners to make the decision. Once the decision is made, practitioners "own" it and can explain the process that led to it. In the words of a doctoral student, "I don't want you to teach me what to do; I

want you to teach me how to think. I will then know what to do."
The purpose is to teach practitioners how to think about ethics;
they will then know what to do.

METHODOLOGY

This book is based on a research study that was motivated by the
paucity of literature on practitioners' awareness, delineation, and
resolution of ethical dilemmas in Jewish communal service. The
aim of the study was to ascertain how practitioners actually think
about ethics, how they wrestle with dilemmas, and how they go
about resolving them.

The preferred method for soliciting responses to these questions was the direct interview. In an interview, questions and
answers can be clarified and probed more deeply. The interviews
turned out to be rich sources of data that revealed the thought
processes, value conflicts, and decisions of the respondents.

A pilot study of ten respondents was initially conducted to
determine whether ethical dilemmas were an issue for practitioners. The findings corroborated the existence of significant dilemmas for social workers, Jewish communal workers, and Jewish
educators. Professionals wanted assistance in identifying, analyzing, and resolving ethical dilemmas in an organized manner. The
results of the pilot study provided the impetus to conduct a second round of in-depth interviews in order to formulate a more
definitive model for the resolution of ethical dilemmas.

This book incorporates six sources of data: the pilot interviews,
the formal interviews, seminars at Jewish communal agencies, the
Ideology course at Wurzweiler, published articles, and social work
practice experiences.

The study was based on the following research question: What
ethical dilemmas are encountered in the field of Jewish communal
service, and how does the professional go about resolving them?
Interviews were conducted with practitioners ranging from
administrators to line workers, in federations, Jewish community
centers, Jewish family and children's agencies, and boards of Jewish education. The pilot sample was selected randomly from
attendees at the Conference of Jewish Communal Service in 1986.
Sample size was deemed to be complete when the subject matter

had been saturated. This occurred when respondents from different settings began to repeat similar ethical themes in the interviews. Theoretical saturation occurs when similar instances appear over and over again and no additional data are being found (Glaser and Strauss 1967, p. 61).

At the outset of the interview, "ethical dilemma" was defined, and the research questions were asked in an open-ended manner. There was a give-and-take during the interviews. Responses were recorded, transcribed, and analyzed according to the theoretical framework. Principles inherent in the respondent's resolution of the dilemma were identified. We refrained from passing judgment on the decision, as the purpose was to provide the theoretical and analytical tools for analyzing and resolving ethical dilemmas.

In the formal study conducted in a large urban setting several years later, three agencies were targeted: a federation, a Jewish family service, and a Jewish community center. More probing questions were asked to ascertain how dilemmas were identified, the degree of stress they caused, with whom staff consulted, and how they went about resolving the dilemmas.

In addition to the formal research, a number of seminars were conducted for the professional staff and board of Jewish Family Services of Baltimore, the New York Association for New Americans, and Hillside Hospital, where values and ethical theory were applied to practice problems. A number of published articles that emanated from those seminars have been adapted for this purpose.

The data were analyzed through content analysis. Principles and theories were inferred from the words and phrases that respondents used to describe the dilemmas. The principles and theories are discussed in Part I, and serve as a framework for the cases discussed in Part II. In the case analyses, mention is made of the antecedent theories, but the focus is on their application to practice problems.

CONTENT AND STRUCTURE

Part I: Theory
The book is divided into two parts. Part I presents a theoretical

framework of professional ethics in Jewish communal service. It contains an analysis of values and ethics, and a comparison between professional ethics and Judaic ethics.

The topics in chapter 1 include the definition, characteristics, and classification of values; conflicts between professional values and client values; and conflicts between personal values and professional values.

Chapter 2 focuses on the relationship between values and ethics; morals and ethics; general ethics and professional ethics; sources of professional ethics; and ethical principles and social work ethics.

Chapter 3 compares Judaic ethics with professional ethics as a way of integrating the Jewish context with the professional function in Jewish communal service.

Part II: Case Illustrations

Chapters in Part II contain case illustrations of ethical dilemmas that derive from different fields of Jewish communal service. Chapters 4 through 7 concentrate on value conflicts. Chapter 4 cites different values regarding agency policy on sexual behavior of cognitively impaired residents of a group home. In chapter 5, the value conflict emerges when a decision needs to be made on placing an elderly couple in a nursing home. Chapter 6 examines conflicts between personal values and professional values in different practice situations. This examination is extended in chapter 7 to priorities in the allocation process, as well as conflicts between personal and professional priorities.

Due to the pervasive influence and critical importance of federations to the continuity of Jewish life, chapters 8 through 12 are devoted to ethical concerns in social planning, fund-raising, allocation of resources, and lay-professional relationships. Chapter 8 discusses the ethical legitimacy of circumventing the waiting list of a nursing home. Ethical issues in fund-raising comprise chapter 9. Chapter 10 is devoted to the distribution process to agencies. This is followed by chapter 11, which applies talmudic reasoning to the financial burdens of resettling Jews from the former Soviet Union.

The Jewish community center, as the agency which serves the social, recreational, and cultural needs of Jewish individuals and families, faces ethical dilemmas that are specific to its operations.

Chapter 12 traces the Jewish component and recent changes in the composition of center professional staff. Ethical dilemmas pit contemporary pluralistic orientations against traditional Jewish values and law. In chapter 13, the autonomy-paternalism conflict surfaces in a center's services to the elderly.

Most Jewish family and children's services are conflicted in serving the intermarried and their families. In chapter 14, ethical concerns are raised by an agency that must decide whether to provide information about Jewish marriage officiators to an engaged interfaith couple, and whether to serve the intermarried at all.

Chapter 15 discusses ethical issues that arise in accepting a child of mixed-married parents into the Jewish school, marketing the Jewish school, teaching content against the school's religious ideology, and central board of Jewish education and federation relationships.

The case illustrations in Part II are located in particular fields of service, but are not necessarily limited to them. For example, the ethics of circumventing the waiting list and dilemmas in fund-raising are discussed in the federation context, but they surface in other Jewish communal agencies as well. Ethical dilemmas that arise in one field of service may also appear in another. Though the specifics of the cases may be different, the analytical model is transferable to other ethical situations.

Chapter 16 discusses problems and prospects regarding the implementation of ethical analysis in Jewish communal service.

Limitations of the study

As society changes, so do its values. Values that are prominent in one period may not be in vogue in another. Managed care has revolutionized the health care system in the past few years. AIDS has transformed social attitudes. The Republican "Contract with America" is challenging traditional values and approaches to social welfare.

As values change, so do ethics. The right or good thing to do is not always the same in every situation. Ethical dilemmas are constantly evolving, and the resolution that was appropriate last time may not be appropriate this time. No research study can possibly encompass all the emerging dilemmas in the course of professional practice and social change. However, the analytic model to be presented can be applied to changing circumstances and newly evolving dilemmas. For this reason analyses of emerging ethical dilemmas on the cutting edge of social change and professional practice will be offered as supplements to this study from time to time.

Relevance to other Religious Groups

Though this study focuses on ethical dilemmas in Jewish communal service, it is not limited to the Jewish community. The analytic process can be applied to ethical dilemmas in communal services sponsored by other religious groups including Catholic Charities and the Protestant Welfare Federations. Each group is interested in preserving its religious values, even as it provides professional services to its clientele. The value conflicts between profession and religion are complex, with no easy resolution, in all religious groups. This study can serve as a model of ethical decision-making generally, but particularly in conflicts between religious and professional values.

PART I

A THEORETICAL FRAMEWORK
FOR PROFESSIONAL ETHICS

Chapter 1

Values

The study of ethical dilemmas in Jewish communal service begins with a theoretical framework for the case analyses that follow in Part II. Part I encompasses the nature and function of values, the relationship between values and ethics, ethical principles and theory, and the interface between professional ethics and Judaic ethics. This chapter deals with the definition, function, and classification of values, conflicts between professional values and client values, and conflicts between personal and professional values. It offers a framework for thinking about values in the professional setting.

DEFINITION

Values "imply a usual preference for certain means, ends, and conditions of life, often being accompanied by strong feeling" (Pumphrey 1959, p. 23). Similar definitions have been made by others (Gordon 1965; Rokeach 1973; Levy 1979; Siporin 1975; National Association of Social Workers 1967). Values carry emotional charges, some more intense than others. In this respect, they differ from casual preferences, which tend to be not as emotionally charged and are more easily discarded. A preference for chocolate over vanilla ice cream can be readily changed when that flavor is not available, compared with a preference for a religious life over a secular life. People make greater personal investments in values that are felt more deeply, and are more abiding. This is due to the fact that values tend to be inculcated during childhood and represent parents' dreams and ideals for their children.

As preferences "with affective regard" (Levy 1979), values need

3

not be testable. They can be asserted without a need to defend or prove them, for they are basically subjective in nature. They differ from knowledge that "refers to what, in fact, seems to be, established by the highest standards of objectivity and rationality of which man is capable" (Gordon 1965, p. 34).

FUNCTIONS

A value-pattern "defines a direction of choice and consequent commitment to action" (Parsons, cited in Levy 1973, p. 36). Values are not merely abstract entities but action-oriented. When many choices of action are available, values lead the individual to choose a specific one and to act upon it (Loewenberg, 1988). Professional values become a source of accountability and evaluation. The "ought" component in values connects values with ethics, which are "values in action" (Levy 1979).

The goals of Jewish social agencies to strengthen Jewish identity, the family, and the Jewish community may be construed as values because these are preferences invested with strong feelings by the sanctioning community, the board of directors, and staff. The agency is expected to offer programs and services designed to achieve these objectives, and can be held accountable by the clientele and the community.

CLASSIFICATION

Values in social work may be classified along three dimensions: (1) as preferred conceptions of people; (2) as preferred outcomes for people; (3) as preferred instrumentalities for dealing with people (Levy 1973). Table 1 classifies values in social work, Judaism, and the professions in Jewish communal service.

Discussion

Social workers function on all three levels shown in the table. On the most abstract level—preferred conceptions—social workers believe that human beings are inherently good, possessing worth, dignity, and the capacity to change. These preferred conceptions serve as the philosophical foundation of the profession. They conduce to what social workers want for people, such as the achieve-

Table 1: Values Classification in Social Work, Judaism, and the Professions in Jewish Communal Service

	Preferred conception of people	Preferred outcome for people	Preferred instrumentalities for dealing with people
Social Workers	inherently good, possess worth and dignity; have capacity to change	meaningful social relationships, needs satisfaction, family life, health, self-actualization	confidentiality, respect, support, empathy, nonjudgmental
Judaism	created in the image of God, infinite value, worth and dignity, capacity to change	moral life, productive family life, repairing the world	performing the commandments, studying the Torah, giving charity, acts of kindness to others
Professionals in Jewish communal service	worth and dignity, capacity for change	strengthening Jewish identity and community	respect, support, empathy, confidentiality, nonjudgmental

ment of meaningful social relationships, healthy family lives, the satisfaction of basic human needs, the repair of person-environment ruptures. How social workers attain these ends is also determined by values. There are preferred ways of working with people, such as respecting their privacy, showing empathy, being nonjudgmental, and offering support.

This classification can be applied to Jewish values. Judaism views human beings as created in the image of God, possessing infinite value and the capacity to change. Preferred outcomes include a moral life, family living, and *tikkun olam*—"repairing the world." Preferred instrumentalities are the mitzvot, such as the study of Torah, *tzedakah* (charity), and *hesed* (kindness), and welcoming strangers—the moral and social values that enable individuals to live in society.

The further one moves down from the level of preferred conceptions, or absolute values, to specific people and conditions—the level of preferred instrumentalities—the more values become relativistic. "Certainly, as one moves toward the earthly levels of everyday life there occurs a loss of purity, an increase of relativism, and often an emergence of conflict between and among values themselves" (Perlman 1976, p. 386).

The professions in Jewish communal service share with social work and Judaism preferred conceptions of people as possessing worth and dignity, and the capacity to change. Some professionals may derive this conception from the ethos of a democratic society, while others may ascribe it to the belief that God created the human being in His own image (Genesis 1:27).

Strengthening Jewish identity and community is a preferred outcome that unites all professions in Jewish communal service. Particular agencies may have additional valued outcomes, such as personality development, marital and family stability, and physical and mental health.

Social workers' preferred ways of working with people—instrumental values—are largely shared by other professionals in Jewish communal service because empathy, respect, and confidentiality are humanistic values. The methods that each profession uses to achieve goals may differ because of its distinct orientations, but they are similar in the three value categories.

PROFESSIONAL VALUES VS. CLIENT VALUES

Social workers believe in people's capacity to change and view themselves as change agents. Change is directed toward helping people improve their level of social functioning and the fit between person and environment (Germain 1991, p. 17).

Clients, too, have values regarding change. They may resist entertaining different ways of coping with their situations. They may dread the consequences of change. A battered wife may opt to remain with her husband because of her dependency needs and the fear of striking out on her own. A group may restrict membership because of the status and friendships already devel--

oped. A community may resist the establishment of a residence for the homeless because of concerns for safety and property values.

Though the resistance to change may be psychologically based, as people are more comfortable with the old and apprehensive about the new, resistance may also stem from traditional cultural values.

The lines of the potential conflict between the social worker and the client can now be drawn. The social worker may be planning a strategy of change for the client, whereas the client may be more tradition-minded and resist change that threatens old and cherished values. The social worker is guided by the client's values, and must be ready "to relinquish his aspirations to effect planned change should his clients prefer not to have it" (Levy 1972, p. 490).

The reverse situation may also occur. The social worker in Jewish communal service may subscribe to values that stem from Jewish tradition, and the client may want to move in a direction that threatens the worker's stance.

In the course of rendering a professional service, the professional's values may clash with the client's values. In Jewish communal service agencies, the executive director's introduction of new policies and procedures may meet resistance from the board, staff, and clientele. Jewishly committed parents whose child is doing poorly in a yeshiva will resist a suggestion to place the child in a public school. Jewish families from the former Soviet Union may be suspicious of a professional's encouragement of greater independence for their adolescent children. An elderly Jewish woman may not want to move out of her apartment in a deteriorating neighborhood. A professional opposed to intermarriage may find it difficult to work with intermarried couples. Psychological and emotional factors may cloud the purity of the values that clients and professionals espouse. The professional must also be aware of the role that Jewish culture, tradition, and religion play in clients' attitudes toward change.

Many of the ethical dilemmas described in Part II derive from conflicts between professional values and client values. While not necessarily involving change, they challenge professionals to determine ways of working with clients whose values differ from theirs.

PERSONAL VALUES VS. PROFESSIONAL VALUES

Another type of value conflict is the clash between personal and professional values. When personal values are not in harmony with professional values, it becomes more difficult to deal with the strain induced by the conflict with the client's values.

Professionals needs to be clear about their personal values. In today's libertarian and relativist moral climate, it has become difficult for many people to be clear about their own values. Many more options are available. A professional needs to know what to believe in and what are deemed to be preferred ways of living and acting (Loewenberg and Dolgoff 1992, p. 51).

A major source of personal-professional value conflict is religion. When personal values stem from religious sources, the professional must be more on guard against their intrusion upon the performance of his or her professional function (Levy 1976*b*, p. 17). These values usually originate in childhood and tend to be deeply embedded in the individual's psyche. The individual feels committed to act upon them and can tolerate little or no deviation.

In the course of their work, practitioners may encounter ideas, values, and situations that are incompatible with their religious beliefs and practices. Where religious values exist minimally or not all, the chances of a serious value clash are reduced. The potential for personal-professional value conflict remains, for practitioners may have strong personal convictions derived from secular sources that could be at odds with the profession's values.

When conflicts between personal/religious values and professional values appear, what is the practitioner to do? How should one go about resolving these conflicts? Danzig (1986, p. 49) posited three strategies.

1. Identification with one's religious commitment.
2. Identification with, and accommodation to, both one's religious and one's social work commitments.
3. Identification with social work as the dominant culture.

The three options for conflict resolution are shown in table 2. The practitioner can prefer religious values over professional values, thus acting unethically from a professional standpoint. At the opposite extreme, the practitioner does not permit personal/religious values to intrude into the professional function. Identification with the profession takes primacy over personal values. The middle option represents an attempt at synthesis. One is true to oneself. There is no denial of religious or professional values, but an effort is made to accommodate both simultaneously. This is accomplished when the practitioner represents, but does not impose, personal values as an alternative to the client's values.

Table 2: Three Options for Conflict Resolution

Personal Values	identification with one's religious commitment	identification with one's religious commitment	
Professional Values		identification with, and accommodation to, one's religious and social work commitments	identification with social work as the dominant culture

Professionals in Jewish communal service also face conflicts between personal values and professional values. The personal values of non-Jewish staff may stem from their religious tradition or from secular sources. As professionals, they are guided by the values of their profession and the values of the Jewish communal agency. Similarly, the personal values of Jewish staff may stem from Jewish tradition or from secular sources. Judaic values appear to be influential in motivating individuals to enter the field of Jewish communal service. Their goals are to strengthen Jewish family life, Jewish identity, and Jewish community. Their commitment to Jewish life is coupled with professional degrees in social work, Jewish communal service, physical education, Jewish education, psychology, Judaic studies, and business administration, among others.

The potential for personal-professional value conflict is greater in the "secular" professions, such as social work, because of the possible disparity between democratic values and Jewish values. The degree of conflict may vary with the degree of religious commitment: the deeper the professional's religious commitment, the greater the possibility of conflict with social work values.

A classic illustration of conflict between personal Jewish values and social work values is the case of a Jewish woman who seeks abortion counseling from an Orthodox Jewish social worker. Where the facts are such that Halakhah (Jewish law) prohibits the abortion, professional values require the social worker to be guided by the client's self-determination. Assuming that the professional's personal values coincide with halakhic values, what should the professional do? How the professional deals with this conflict indicates whether religious commitment, professional commitment, or their integration is the primary strategy of negotiation among conflicting values.

Orthodox Catholics face similar conflicts. A homosexual dying of AIDS asked a Jesuit priest to stand with him as he tried to talk to his parents. The priest writes: "Church law forbids homosexual acts, however, and according to the rules, I should have condemned him. But I stood with Bobby and helped his parents accept him as I was also learning to do" (Burns 1987, p. 6). These two cases portray the conflict between a professional's personal values—the religious prohibition against abortion in the first case, against homosexuality in the second—and the imperative to be sensitive to client needs.

CONCLUSION

Values, as strongly felt preferences, point in the direction of action. They can be classified into preferred conceptions of viewing people, preferred outcomes of what we want for people, and preferred instrumentalities of the ways we work with people. Conflicts between professional and client values, and between personal and professional values exist on various levels in Jewish communal service. Conflicts are especially troublesome between Jewish values and professional values because agencies and professionals subscribe to both. Conflicts in values inevitably lead to ethical dilemmas. The next chapter deals with ethics in professional practice.

Chapter 2

Ethics

In chapter 1, we defined and classified values, and analyzed value conflicts between professionals and clients, and between personal and professional values. Now we define ethics and morals, trace the rationale for, and sources of, professional ethics, and relate ethical principles to social work values. These chapters serve as a theoretical base for the cases that follow in Part II.

DEFINITION

An essential characteristic of values is that they commit the individual to action. The action which is the ethics is imbedded in values, but not all values become ethics. Those values that represent normative standards of behavior become ethics when they are converted into action. This is what is meant by "ethics is values in action" (Levy 1979, p. 9). The preference is the value; the action upon the preference is the ethics. The preference (value) leads to the moral action (ethics). The moral obligation to act upon the value inheres in the value and is socially confirmed by the prevailing normative standards of behavior.

Ethics comes into play only in relationship. "The concept ethics is limited here to conduct arising from specific interpersonal relationships" (Levy 1976*a*, p. 27). Epictetus said it long ago: "Our duties are in general measured by our social relationships. He is a father. One is called upon to take care of him" (cited in Johnson 1984, p. 96). The responsibility to act in an ethical manner derives from social relationships. Ethical obligations derive from relationships between friends, married couples, parents and children, professionals and clients, employers and employees. Duties

11

defined by interpersonal relationships differ from ethical responsibilities regulated by law, and apply even if not regulated.

ETHICS AND MORALS

Though the terms "ethics" and "morals" tend to be used interchangeably, they are not synonymous. Ethics is the system or code; morals are the standards of behavior that are codified in ethics. Ethics is the theoretical examination of the practice of morality (Webster 1964).

In this study, ethics differ from morals in that ethics inhere in relationships, whereas morals refer to standards of conduct in society (Levy 1976a, p. 27). *The assessment of conduct on the basis of general social norms is in the category of morality. The assessment of conduct arising from specific interpersonal relationships is in the category of ethics.*

As an illustration, infidelity is immoral behavior that is judged according to normative standards in society. When considered within a specific marital relationship, infidelity is also unethical.

Jewish communal professionals have the same moral obligations as other people, but they also have ethical obligations by virtue of their relationships with their constituents. The term "morals" will be used when reference is made to general standards of professional behavior. "Ethics" will be used to describe professional actions in the social service relationship.

GENERAL ETHICS VS. PROFESSIONAL ETHICS

Professional codes of ethics seem to be superfluous when ethics already exist in the family and in the broader society. Everyday morality, such as honesty, trustworthiness, and keeping promises, should be a sufficient basis for prescribing the conduct of all people, including professionals. Why the need for professional ethics? (Goldman 1980).

In the family, the values of care and children's dependency obligate parents to care for children (Levy 1982, p. 15). Ethical responses can take two forms: passive and active. One ought not to take advantage of the other in a dependency relationship. One also has a responsibility to provide care for a dependent person.

Ethical obligations to care for dependent persons can be

applied to adult children and elderly parents (Callahan 1985). The twofold obligation requires children not to take undue advantage of their elderly parents and to provide for their needs. Dependency at both ends of the chronological spectrum evokes ethical duties for parents to their children, and for adult children to their elderly parents (Linzer 1987).

In social work, client dependency and client vulnerability obligate professionals to constrain their own behavior and to offer services for client protection (Lewis 1986, p. 16). The first principle of ethics is to do no harm. In Jewish communal service, some settings are more conducive to serving vulnerable clients and some to serving dependent clients. When clients come to the agency, the professional becomes ethically responsible for doing no harm and for providing services that will meet their needs.

In comparing parent-child and professional-client relationships, general ethics and professional ethics share two things in common. Values commit to ethical duties, and the dependency and vulnerability of one evoke an ethical obligation in the other.

Though values and dependency conduce to ethical obligations in general society and in the professions, a case can be made for professional ethics independent of general ethics because of the distinctive character of the professions (Levy 1979; Loewenberg and Dolgoff 1992). Caplan (1986) offers three factors in support of professional ethics: moral uncertainty, autonomy, and special moral relationships.

Moral uncertainty exists when one system of morality cannot be applied to all ambiguous situations. As an example, general morality cannot guide medical practice in the case of euthanasia. Apparently, society has decided to transfer the painful decision of euthanasia to the medical profession because of the moral uncertainty involved.

Autonomy, a central theme in the literature of professional ethics (Callahan 1985), cannot be supported at all costs and in all situations; it is not an absolute value. There are clients who prefer to "dump" their autonomy into the professional's lap. "You know best" captures this mentality. Incompetent people cannot exercise autonomy. Professionals would seem to be justified in acting on what they deem to be in the client's best interests to prevent immediate harm and to restore autonomy (Caplan 1986).

It is reasonable to expect that people who possess special knowledge or skill would have ethical duties to those who seek their services. "Specialization and inequities in the distribution of knowledge and training are the moral foundations for professional ethics" (Caplan 1986, p. 12). Greater knowledge and skill obligate professionals to behave in particular ways with clients. Moral uncertainty, autonomy, and special moral relationships legitimate the rationale for distinctive codes of professional ethics.

SOURCES OF PROFESSIONAL ETHICS

The two main questions of ethics, how to determine what is right and how to determine what is good, evolved into two traditions. The first, deontology, is concerned with moral obligation or duty; the second, teleology, with the ends or purposes of action.

The Deontological Tradition

In the deontological tradition, common sense (Ross 1930) and intuition (Bradley, cited in Johnson 1984, p. 295) denote some types of action as right and others as wrong. It is self-evident that we ought to return a borrowed book simply because we borrowed it. The moral "ought", unconditional and binding, was designated by Kant as the "categorical imperative" (Kant, cited in Johnson 1984, p. 199).

The concept of prima facie duties can assist in determining the right ethical action (Ross, cited in Johnson 1965). Prima facie duty refers to an act which is fitting or appropriate to the situation at the time. There is a prima facie duty to keep a promise—fidelity. This duty rests on a previous act—having made a promise—that requires no justification other than being the commonsensical thing to do in the situation. Other prima facie duties include:

1. Those resting on a previous wrongful act—reparation.
2. Those resting on previous acts that others did to the individual—gratitude.
3. Those resting on a distribution of pleasure or happiness—justice.
4. Those making the lot of other people better—beneficence.
5. Those improving our own condition—self-improvement.

6. Those not injuring others—nonmaleficence.

When there is a conflict between prima facie duties, it is necessary to study the situation as fully as possible until an opinion is formed that one action is more incumbent than the other. "Then I am bound to think that to do this *prima facie* duty is my duty in the situation" (Ross, cited in Johnson 1965, p. 401). Ross offers neither principles nor rules to guide the individual in establishing priorities. This stance has considerable bearing on the resolution of ethical dilemmas.

As an illustration, service to parents is a prima facie duty of gratitude, whereas the care of children is a prima facie duty of beneficence (Wurzburger 1984). When these duties clash, i.e., when an adult child is caught between the demands of elderly parents and dependent children, the individual needs to determine which duty is more incumbent in the situation, and act accordingly. At times, the duty to parents will be stronger, and at times the duty to children will take priority (Linzer 1986a). There is no infallible rule to guide individuals in all situations.

Deontological tradition posits the intrinsic awareness of the rightness of an act (Beauchamp and Childress 1989). Intuitively, we know what we ought to do in a particular situation, and need not look to the consequences in order to determine the ethical imperative.

The Teleological Tradition

The teleological tradition in ethics is primarily known as utilitarianism. The theory of utility, or the greater happiness principle, affirms that "actions are right in proportion as they tend to promote happiness, wrong as they tend to produce the reverse of happiness" (Mill, cited in Johnson 1985, p. 264). The teleological or utilitarian tradition deems an action good if it leads to good results for a great number of people. The ethics of an act can only be determined by its consequences.

We resort to both utilitarian theory and deontological theory to guide practitioners in ethical decision-making. One may ask the purpose of having two theories if they lead to the same results. For example, both deontologists and utilitarians contend that promises should be kept, though for different reasons. The answer is that there are situations where the outcomes may differ. For example, in many states the law requires that suspected child abuse be reported to the proper authorities. A deontologically oriented social worker would file a report because it is the right thing to do. A utilitarian social worker might not, because of the possible negative consequences, reasoning that reporting might retard the client's therapeutic progress or that the client might leave the agency (Reamer 1982*a*). But reporting could also lead to a greater good, such as saving the child's life. Operationalizing both theories is complex because plausible arguments could be offered to justify taking opposite stances in an ethical dilemma.

The deontological position reflects moral imperatives that are inherently correct. The utilitarian position offers more leeway for ethical exploration because of the indeterminacy of anticipating consequences and defining the greater good.

Social Work Ethics

Since many professionals in Jewish communal service are social workers, and more has been written about social work ethics than the ethics of other professions in Jewish communal service, we will concentrate on the theoretical underpinnings of social work ethics.

Deontology and utilitarianism can both serve as the bases for social work ethics. Levy adopts the deontological approach. "Ethics, in effect, is a function of the relationship between parties to any transaction, and the responsibilities which inhere in that relationship" (Levy 1982, p. 1). The functional relationship between the social worker and the client forms the basis of ethical activity (Nulman 1984). It is the context, and not the consequences, of the professional relationship that determines the ethical imperative of the social worker (Levy 1974*b*, p. 74).

Reamer (1982*a*) finds serious weaknesses with each theory. Lewis (1984) supports both theories in making ethical assessments. Utilitarianism is likely to yield a tentative choice of action that can be revised when new information changes the service situation. The deontological approach requires the social worker to reason from general ethical imperatives to guide the specific instance. The social worker may choose either approach but needs to be consistent.

In sum, professional ethics can be traced to two philosophical traditions—the deontological and the utilitarian. There are situations where both theories lead to the same action and situations where they lead to different actions. The practitioner has a choice of theory to justify ethical actions.

Practitioners who are not social workers can acquire the thinking process and tools of ethical analysis from the exposition of social work ethics. They could then adapt it to their practice.

THE ROLE OF ETHICAL PRINCIPLES IN DECISION-MAKING

Ethical analysis and decision-making are necessary when practitioners are faced with ethical dilemmas. Ethical dilemmas constitute the bulk of the case examples in Part II. An ethical dilemma is defined as a choice between two actions that are based on conflicting values. Both values are morally correct and professionally grounded, but they cannot be acted upon together in the situation. Both of them are right and good, and that is what causes the dilemma for the practitioner. The decision on which course of action to take should not be intuitive, but should be based on a logical, reasoned approach.

Theory alone does not suffice to justify ethical action because it is too abstract and unspecific. Intermediate steps are needed. Beauchamp and Childress (1994, p. 15) posit a deductive model of justification diagrammed as follows:

4. Ethical Theory
3. Principles
2. Rules
1. Particular Judgments

Particular judgments are required in ethically ambiguous situations. The professional practitioner can justify the decision by resorting to a rule that guides the action. The rule can be justified by resorting to a principle. All three can be supported by an ethical theory.

As an example, a nurse who refuses to assist in an abortion could justify her decision by citing the rule that it is wrong to kill an innocent human being intentionally. The rule itself can be justified by resorting to the principle of respect for the sanctity of life. The decision, rule, and principle can be supported by deontological or utilitarian theory.

By utilizing this model, the professional can defend the decision as ethically correct in the face of opposition. Though the model does not mention values as sources of justification, they are implicit in the rules and principles. This model will be utilized in Part II to analyze ethical dilemmas. The analysis incorporates rules, principles, and theories to justify ethical action, with an emphasis on principles and theories.

ETHICAL PRINCIPLES OF AUTONOMY AND BENEFICENCE

In the framework of utilitarian and deontological theory, two important ethical principles are utilized to justify professional practice in Jewish communal settings: autonomy and beneficence. Table 3 portrays the theoretical supports for these principles, and their application to social work practice.

Table 3: Ethical principles supported by ethical theories, applied to social work practice

Ethical Principles	Ethical Theories		Social Work Practice
	Deontology	Utilitarianism	
Autonomy	People possess unconditional worth; right to determine their own destiny	people to develop their own potential in the future	self-determination; client's right to make decisions affecting one's life
Beneficence (Paternalism)	"reciprocity theory of obligations"—in response to others' kindness	leads to improved living conditions and better society	agency responsible for client's welfare; Jewish community as a counter value to self-determination

The Principle of Respect for Autonomy

The core of the concept of autonomy refers to the rule of the self free from control by others and from personal limitations that prevent meaningful choice. By contrast, a person of limited autonomy is in some respects controlled by others or incapable of acting on his or her own. Autonomy may be restricted only if it is necessary to prevent harm to other people. If the restriction is justified, it must rest on a competing moral principle, such as beneficence or justice.

The Principle of Beneficence

Morality requires not only that we treat people autonomously and refrain from harming them, but that we contribute to their welfare. These actions fall under the principle of beneficence.

General obligations of beneficence, or the "reciprocity theory of obligations" (Beauchamp and Childress 1989), are in response to the benefits we receive from others. Specific obligations of beneficence derive from the special moral relationships inhering in such social roles as parent, spouse, and friend. Human needs usually form the basis of the beneficent relationship (Beauchamp and Childress 1989).

Beneficence and Paternalism

The principle of beneficence is often allied with paternalism. Paternalism is the overriding of a person's wishes or actions, through coercion, deception, lying, or nondisclosure of information, for beneficent reasons. It is not considered paternalism when a professional overrides a client's autonomy in order to prevent harm to others or the violation of moral principles.

Paternalism occurs when the professional refuses to agree to the client's wishes when no one else is involved, merely because the professional disagrees with the client's values. This is considered an affront to the dignity and independence of the client (Linzer and Lowenstein 1987). Childress (1981) argues that paternalism is prima facie wrong and needs to be justified.

Abramson (1985, 1989) cites four situations in which paternalism is justified: (1) acting on behalf of a child who is too young to make decisions; (2) treating a person who is mentally incompetent; (3) preventing an irreversible act, such as suicide; and (4) temporarily interfering with a person's liberty so as to ensure future freedom and autonomy.

Paternalism directly confronts the principle of autonomy. Should the principle of respect for client autonomy have priority over the principle of professional beneficence? The conflict between these principles is uneven. Due to the popularity of the autonomy model, it is difficult to find clear commitments to the beneficence model. Beauchamp and Childress (1989, p. 211), who seem to support beneficence, conclude that neither principle can override the other.

Callahan questions the supremacy of autonomy over such considerations as community. As a system of values for individual welfare, autonomy may be the answer. But as a system of values for life in community, autonomy may not do as well. Autonomy "will inevitably diminish the sense of obligation that others may feel toward us and shrivel our sense of obligation toward others" (Callahan 1984, p. 40). When we juxtapose autonomy with community, we introduce constraints and limits, and a vision of the self that is part of a wider collectivity. Autonomy is *a* value, not *the* value.

Each principle can be independently supported by both deontology and utilitarianism. When they confront each other, i.e., when autonomy is juxtaposed with beneficence, they carry equal weight. In supporting autonomy, the focus is on the client; in supporting beneficence, the focus is on the agency and the community. When beneficence turns into paternalism, i.e., the action overrides the client's wishes for the client's own good, autonomy usually has the upper hand, and is difficult to overrule.

ETHICAL PRINCIPLES AND SOCIAL WORK VALUES

Among the value conflicts that permeate social work practice in Jewish communal service are client self-determination vs. agency responsibility, and professional values vs. Jewish values. The common denominator is the wishes of the client vs. the constraints of the agency and community. Freedberg (1989, p. 33) has framed this conflict as a "balance between responsibility to the community and responsibility to the self-determination of the individual client system." Self-determination implies individual rights and the capacity to direct one's life, and is synonymous with the ethical principle of autonomy.

Neither self-determination nor autonomy is absolute. Each is circumscribed by the natural limits of outer reality, the infringement on others' self-determination and autonomy, and causing harm to oneself. Not everyone wishes to assert autonomy or is capable of doing so (Caplan 1986). Despite these qualifications, self-determination and autonomy are weighty principles that can be countered only by weighty counterprinciples.

Community as a Counterprinciple

Community (Callahan 1984), and Jewish community in particular, may be one such counterprinciple to autonomy. The Jewish social agency, sanctioned by the Jewish community, reflects the community's values. The local Jewish community, with its array of religious, social, cultural, and educational institutions, serves as a sacred canopy that strengthens the belonging and identity of individuals, groups, and families. The value of community is supported by the "Communitarians," a group of social thinkers who "emphasize the importance of community, the moral claims staked by shared needs and futures, as distinct from the claims of various subgroups and individuals" (Etzioni 1991, p. A-22). Community is another part of external reality with which clients must contend when they come to the agency for service. The professional can use it as a counterbalance to client self-determination and autonomy.

CONCLUSION

The theoretical framework for professional ethics encompasses their definition, origins, and principles. It is designed to provide professionals with the tools for ethical decision-making. These tools include determining the respective values, and the rules, principles, and theories to justify the respective actions. It offers a systematic way of thinking about ethics to help professionals avoid instinctive responses to complex conflict situations. Professional ethics and Judaic ethics will now be compared to illuminate some of the dilemmas in Jewish communal service.

Chapter 3

Professional Ethics and Jewish Ethics

In the preceding chapter, theoretical frameworks for professional ethics and social work ethics were presented. We now turn to the nature of Jewish ethics and Jewish law, Jewish ethics in a pluralistic Jewish community, the interface between professional ethics and Jewish ethics, and conflicts between professional values and Jewish values in Jewish communal service.

JEWISH ETHICS AND JEWISH LAW

Jewish ethics may be defined as Judaism's teachings about moral issues. For those familiar with the all-embracing character of Halakhah, or Jewish law, there would seem to be no independent Jewish ethics since ethical conduct is incorporated into Halakhah. In order to distinguish between Jewish law and Jewish ethics, it may be helpful in our discussion to limit the halakhic system to behavioral obligations and the Jewish ethical system to character development and personal virtues (Wurzburger, 1994).

Jacobs (1969, pp. 9–10) offers four distinctions between Jewish law and Jewish ethics. (1) Law is concerned with minimum standards, whereas ethics demands rising above the bare minimum. (2) Law provides rules for all, whereas ethics is more individualistic, encouraging the realization of each person's potential. (3) In law the emphasis is on action; ethics, though concerned with action, tends to emphasize the formation of character. (4) Jewish law is deeply rooted in Jewish history and speaks primarily to Jews, whereas ethics speaks to the human being with human needs. Despite these distinctions, to committed Jews, Jewish ethics is indistinguishable from Halakhah, which encompasses behavior,

23

character, and mind-set (Soloveitchik 1983).

Jewish ethics is based in the Torah and amplified in the Talmud. It flourished during the medieval period in the writings of Moses Maimonides, Bahya Iba Paquda, Judah ben Samuel HeHasid, and Moses ben Jacob Cordovero. An important outgrowth of medieval Jewish ethics was the Musar movement of the nineteenth century, led by Rabbi Israel Salanter.

The literature of medieval Jewish ethics was addressed to people who, until the end of the eighteenth century, were not recognized by any European country as full-fledged citizens with civil rights. The concern of Jewish ethics was how to help Jews to develop their moral character to its fullest capacity within their self-enclosed communities.

With the spread of Enlightenment, when they were accepted as citizens of their European countries, Jews were confronted with a new problem: how to remain Jewish while participating in Western civilization. Contemporary Jewish ethics is distinguished from medieval Jewish ethics in that the problems it faces are largely the same ones that confront the surrounding culture. As Jews interact with the larger society, the society's moral concerns influence Jewish thought and behavior.

Four responses to contemporary moral concerns have evolved. They are represented in the major religious movements in the Jewish community: Orthodoxy, Reform, Conservatism, and Reconstructionism. As a result of this diversity, one cannot ask for *the* Jewish position on a topic, for there is no one Jewish position. This has considerable impact on resolving ethical dilemmas in Jewish communal service.

IDEOLOGICAL DIFFERENCES

Kellner (1978) ascribes the basic theological differences among the four Jewish religious movements to their conceptions of revelation. Orthodoxy believes that the Torah represents the direct revelation of God's will. Halakhah, as the will of God, is normative for all Jews at all times. Orthodoxy recognizes halakhic change, but holds that it may come about only within the Halakhah's own legal mechanisms. It is not subject to the historical development that is characteristic of human institutions.

Reform Judaism rejects the divinity of the Halakhah and believes that revelation is akin to inspiration. Reform is concerned with ethics, and insists that ethical monotheism is the essential character of Judaism. While there have been many modifications of the Pittsburgh Platform since 1885, Reform Judaism still rejects the Halakhah as a norm and looks to the prophetic tradition for the essence of Judaism. There are doubts about the reality of specific revelations and the authority of commandments. Personal autonomy and freedom to choose are Reform's norms (*Jewish Week* 1993). "Humanism and secularism have made deep inroads into traditional categories of thought. . . . It is doubtful that there are final and fixed conclusions any more. Revelation is in the encounter" (Silver 1970, pp. 4, 6).

Conservative Judaism occupies the middle position between Orthodoxy and Reform. It believes that the Torah was written by divinely inspired men. Halakhah is the way in which Jews have sought to preserve their experiences of God. Judaism is basically a human institution that undergoes change and historical development like all human institutions. Conservative Judaism sees the Halakhah as normative but not absolute.

Reconstructionism, an offshoot of Conservatism, similarly rejects the Halakhah as God's will and views Judaism as an evolving religious civilization. Judaism's laws are part of its larger culture, subject to change and development in interaction with the surrounding culture. To facilitate our analysis, Reconstructionism will be incorporated into Conservatism.

These diverse interpretations of revelation and Halakhah give rise to different emphases within Jewish ethics. In general, Orthodox thinkers such as Bleich (1981) approach questions of ethics by applying the teachings of the Halakhah. Orthodox thinkers will not admit the possibility of contradiction between an ethical teaching and the Halakhah.

Contradiction, however, is a distinct possibility among Conservative thinkers. Siegel (1971, pp. 33–34) argues that "according to our interpretation of Judaism, the ethical values of our tradition should have power to judge the particulars of Jewish law. If any law in our tradition does not fulfill our ethical values, then the law should be abolished or revised."

Reform shifts discussions on ethics from specifics, as found in the Responsa literature, to broad invocations of the passion of biblical prophecy. Silver (1970), however, claims that while precision was the great virtue of the rabbinic ethical stance and passion permeates current ethical activity, passion does not suffice; law is necessary. "If the Halakhah and the casuistic method are abrogated, how does anyone get down to specifics?" (ibid., p. 6). Resolution of the conflict between law and ethics appears to be of concern to Reform thinkers.

PLURALISM IN THE JEWISH COMMUNITY

The three denominational approaches to Jewish ethics reflect the state of pluralism in the Jewish community. Pluralism implies the existence of diverse groups that comprise the population of a country. Cultural pluralism anticipates groups living in cooperation, harmony, and mutual respect, comprising a democracy of nationalities.

Religious pluralism emerged from the secularization of traditional religion. Secularization is the process by which sectors of society and culture are removed from the domination of religious institutions and symbols. Secularizing tendencies affect the totality of cultural life. They can be observed in the decline of religious content in the arts, philosophy, and literature, and in using science as an autonomous perspective on the world (Berger 1967, p. 107).

The Jewish community has been unalterably affected by secularization and pluralism. The rise of the non-Orthodox denominations—Reform, Conservatism, and Reconstructionism—reflects the growing secularization of traditional Judaism and the emergence of a pluralistic Jewish culture. "Growing out of the interplay between processes of modernity, secularization, and traditional Judaism, these movements have evolved paths that diverge from traditional Judaism in belief, practice, interpretation, and application of Jewish law (Halakhah)" (Levine 1987, p. 30). Levine continues (p. 31):

> We are also learning that each movement in Judaism is itself composed of a range of subgroupings, representing shades of practice, social attitudes, beliefs, orientations to Jewish law, etc. Generally, Orthodoxy would not support pluralist approaches to Judaism,

which they would consider deviant and unfaithful to the dictates of the Torah, God and the Revelation at Sinai as described in the Bible. Yet, to an extent, a pluralism within the Orthodox movement seems to be emerging, creating tensions and trends of polarization similar to those which characterize the Jewish community at large.

Recognizing these pluralistic trends as a harbinger of irreconcilable splits in the Jewish community, Greenberg has called for interdenominational dialogue to search out the common ground for building unity amid diversity. "All sides must come to a deeper understanding of the implications of pluralism. Pluralism means more than allowing others to do and believe things which one cannot accept. Pluralism implies that people must accept limits for the sake of living together" (Greenberg 1986, p. 25). Greenberg urges each denomination to bend on the firm stand it has taken on matters of personal status, divorce, etc., and search for ways to arrive at a consensus for the sake of promoting unity in *Klal Yisrael*—the Jewish community.

JEWISH COMMUNAL SERVICE

For many Jews, Jewish ethics derives from biblical and classical Judaic sources, with differences in the application of these sources to modern ethical situations. For other Jews, modern Jewish ethics stems from Jewish civil religion. The Holocaust and the State of Israel are two major sources for ethical action. Emil Fackenheim's 614th commandment—do not give Hitler a posthumous victory— serves as a source of ethical action. It exhorts Jews to be committed to Jewish living, to acquire a Jewish education, to marry other Jews, and to raise a family. The State of Israel beckons Jews to identify with other Jews, give charity, care for Jewish refugees and immigrants, and promote the unity of Jews the world over. Though professionals in Jewish communal service embrace different sources of Jewish ethics, they are united in trying to strengthen Jewish identity and community.

As the role and function of Jewish communal service has changed historically from "Americanizing" Jews to "Judaizing" Americans, so has there been a shift from the predominance of social work as the host profession, with its primary concern for individual well-being, to multi-disciplines and their primary concern with Jewish group survival. When social work was the host profession, agency ambience, philosophy, programs, and services were permeated by the emphasis on individual development, family growth, and the fit between person and environment. With the current emphasis on Jewish continuity, the survival of the group is deemed more important than the growth of the individual. Individual needs are superseded by communal needs, and self-determination is of secondary importance to community welfare.

The emphasis on community has been given greater prominence through Solomon's proposed "Ethical Ten Commandments" (1994), designed to unify the various professional disciplines in Jewish communal service.

I.   Thou shalt begin with the foundation of Torah, Avodah, and Gemilut Chassadim.
II.   Thou shalt build community.
III. Thou shalt participate in the aspiration of the Jewish people by helping to build a homeland in Israel.
IV.   Thou shalt respect the diversity of this people by standing in the place of all Jews of all denominations and beliefs.
V.   Thou shalt seek excellence in all of your work in the community.
VI.   Thou shalt seek to transmit Jewish values.
VII. Thou shalt act with respect for all thy colleagues working in behalf of the community.
VIII. Thou shalt advocate those values of human and social justice which make us a light unto the nations.
IX.   Thou shalt educate the community through thy work.
X.   Thou shalt educate thyself through continued Jewish learning.

These "commandments" direct each professional to look beyond individual needs to further the needs of the Jewish community. Professionals not oriented to individual development experience no overt conflict between the ideology of Jewish agencies and the values of their professions. They can readily adapt to the primacy of communal values, and orient their services accordingly. The conflict emerges when Jewish communal values are compared with social work values. Ideological conflict between social work values and Jewish values is exacerbated for social workers in Jewish communal service.

The ideological conflicts analyzed through the case method in Part II include client self-determination and agency commitment to Jewish continuity; the social worker's personal Jewish values and the client's difference with those values; personal needs vs. professional obligations to the Jewish community; serving the general community and the Jewish community; developing a policy on homosexuality in a Jewish community center; accepting the child of a non-Jewish mother into an Orthodox Jewish day school; developing a policy on sexual behavior in group homes for cognitively disabled persons; formulating a policy on serving the intermarried in Jewish family services; a teen basketball team playing in a league on the Sabbath. The diversity in these conflicts can be located, with some exceptions, in clashes between Jewish traditional values and laws, represented by professionals and agencies, and the needs and life-styles of clients who do not conform to these values and laws. Social workers committed to Jewish, agency, and client values need to determine whether compromises are possible or whether sides must be taken. The ultimate decision may be fraught with the discomfort of having to choose between two goods, leaving moral traces in the decision not taken.

The field of Jewish communal service consists of a multiplicity of agency settings where a wide variety of professional practice takes place. As entities under Jewish auspices, these agencies can be termed "Jewish agencies," not only because they serve and are funded by Jews, but because they stand for Jewish values and are committed to Jewish continuity. Since values are imperatives to action, agencies are ethically bound to translate their Jewish values into programs and services that reflect those values.

Jewish agencies usually reflect the value orientations of the communities they serve. Ideological diversity and pluralism in the Jewish community conduce to differences regarding the primacy and ethical imperatives of Jewish values. Lay persons and professionals who identify with the different value systems of the Jewish religious movements may legitimately disagree on the right action required in a particular situation. When professional ethics interface with Jewish ethics, the issues become more complex and the potential for conflict is rife, owing to the distinct frameworks that professional and Jewish ethics represent.

CONCLUSION

Jewish ethics and social work ethics represent two systems of thought that interface in professional practice in Jewish communal service. In the case analyses that follow in Part II, social work values and ethics are juxtaposed with the Jewish ideological diversity that exists among professionals and laity in the Jewish community. Conflicts ensue for social workers who need to negotiate between the Jewish and social work systems in deciding how to resolve value conflicts and ethical dilemmas.

PART II

CASE ILLUSTRATIONS OF VALUE CONFLICTS AND ETHICAL DILEMMAS

Chapter 4

The Role of Values in Determining Agency Policy

Members of the staff of the Jewish Family Services of Baltimore had been discussing the ethics of their agency's policy on the sexual behavior of persons with mental retardation in group homes (Howard et al. 1991). The question posed in the article was: "What kind of sexual behavior would the agency accept by residents in the group homes, and under what conditions?" Staff members wanted to know what the agency policy should be on this matter, and whether the policy was ethical. Ethics, defined as "values in action" (Levy 1979), represents action that is consistent with values that reflect general moral standards. This chapter analyzes the values of agency policy with regard to the sexual behavior of persons with mental retardation in its group homes. In a broader sense, it highlights the role of values in determining agency policy.

CATEGORIES OF PROFESSIONAL VALUES

In chapter 1, professional values were classified into three groups: preferred conceptions of people, preferred outcomes for people, and preferred instrumentalities for working with people (Levy 1973).

The first category of professional values informs and influences the others. How we prefer to view people determines the outcomes we want for them, and the ways in which we work in order to achieve these outcomes. The worth and dignity of human beings and their capacity for change are examples of preferred

33

conceptions in social work. If we view people as possessing dignity and worth, we want them to live in dignity. Outcomes include good health, a home, a job, a decent income, self-fulfillment, family life, and so on. Preferred instrumentalities refer to how social workers work with people. Social workers value being nonjudgmental, nondiscriminating, while providing support and maintaining confidentiality. These practice values reflect respect for human potential and help people achieve dignity in their life.

Although other parties, such as state government, are interested in the sexual-behavior policy issue, social workers, parents, and the Jewish community were selected for the focus of this chapter. Their respective positions are discussed at length in the next three sections and presented in abbreviated form in table 4.

Table 4: Values Classification by Three Major Parties to the Agency Policy on Sexual Behavior

	Preferred Conceptions of People	Preferred Outcomes for People	Preferred Instrumentalities for Working with People
Social Worker	Dignity Capacity for self-actualization	Empowerment Happiness Fulfillment	Self-determination Non-judgmental Protection from exploitation
Parents	Dependency Needing protection	Safety Protection Happiness	Supervised environment Setting limits Education
Judaism	Dignity Capacity to abide by Jewish law	Refrain from sexual behavior conformity to Jewish law	Supervised environment Setting limits Education

The clients were not included because of their special relationship to the values issue in question. In other words, the client is the object of values of the other parties whose preferred conceptions, outcomes, and instrumentalities affect the client. Clients in this situation are adults over the age of 21 who are legally responsible for their own decision-making. According to state law, their parents are no longer their guardians.

Maryland state law guarantees the right of group residents to sexual expression, but the state does not define its meaning. Insofar as the agency is licensed and funded by the state, the contractual obligation to meet these regulations supersedes other considerations. Considerable pressure is imposed on the staff and board to abide by these regulations.

SOCIAL WORKERS

Social workers, guided by their professional values, view individuals with cognitive disabilities as human beings who possess dignity, worth, and feelings, are capable of self-fulfillment, and have the right to personal happiness. Just as gradations of ability exist among human beings in general, gradations of intelligence, decision-making, and self-fulfillment occur among individuals with mental disabilities.

From the social worker's standpoint, the preferred outcomes for this group include empowerment, happiness, and self-fulfillment. These outcomes are based on the social worker's education, training, and knowledge of individuals' capacities for reasoning and intimacy—values that social workers help their clients translate into action.

Social workers' preferred instrumentalities include remaining nonjudgmental and supporting client self-determination. Both of these practice values support freedom of sexual expression insofar as individuals with cognitive disabilities are capable of informed consent. Such freedoms are limited by the ability of individuals to assume responsibility for their sexual behavior and its consequences. This practice value encourages self-expression and decision-making.

PARENTS

Parents of adult children with mental disabilities prefer to view them as dependent persons who need protection and do not have the same sexual drives as others. To be sure, parents perceive the worth, dignity, and feelings of their children. Nevertheless, they relegate the sexual drives of their adult children to a category different from other drives, such as hunger and thirst. "Parents, professionals, and community members often view persons with mental retardation as non-sexual" (Howard et al. 1991, p. 363).

Parents' preferred outcomes are directly related to their preferred conceptions of their children. They would like the agency to ensure their children's safety and protect them from possible harmful consequences of group living, including pregnancy, AIDS, and physical injury. Although they want their children to be happy in the group home, their view of such happiness does not entail sexual activity.

Parents value the supervised environment and the education for daily living provided by the home. They view the home as an institution of social control, an agent of the community, whose mission is to protect their children from the outside world and to serve as a substitute for their role as caregivers. Therefore, parents prefer that the home provide the limits and the care that they had provided when their child was at home.

JEWISH COMMUNITY

For Jewish Family Services, defining the term "Jewish" is a policy dilemma. The Orthodox Jewish community would like to append a religious definition to the term, thus requiring the agency to abide by Jewish religious values and laws. The majority of the Jewish community, however, views the agency as sociologically Jewish, serving a broad range of Jews who are ideologically diverse. With regard to this issue, the majority believes that Jewish Family Services should be denominationally neutral and not identify with the values of only one branch of Judaism.

Because the Orthodox Jewish community is influential in the larger Jewish community and in the agency, its ideological stance is represented in table 4. The Orthodox community prefers to view individuals with cognitive disabilities as possessing dignity and as being capable of abiding by Jewish law. They are believed to have the capacity to perform mitzvot and to control their impulses as required by Jewish law.

The Orthodox Jewish community would like the group-home

residents to control their sexual behavior outside marriage with the help, as needed, of agency professionals. Residents' conformity to the Jewish sex ethic is a priority value. The Orthodox community would like all institutions supported by Jewish communal funds to conform to such values.

Its preferred instrumental values include providing a supervised environment, setting limits, and education for self-control. These values are similar to those of the parents.

IMPLICATIONS FOR JEWISH FAMILY SERVICES

This analysis occurs within the context of Maryland state law, which supports sexual behavior by mentally disabled adults. It reveals a fundamental conflict in values for the social worker, parents, and the Orthodox Jewish community. Professional social work values the innate worth and capacity of individuals with mental disabilities and wants them to achieve self-fulfillment and happiness according to their capabilities. To arrive at these ends, social workers value self-determination and a nonjudgmental stance within an environment that protects clients from exploitation. Social workers who are educated about mental disabilities support the right of people with mental disabilities to engage in consenting sexual activities. They attempt to help them clarify their values and make informed educated decisions.

Parental values and Orthodox Jewish communal values coincide with regard to their preferred view of persons with mental disabilities as being limited in their capacities. Consequently, both preferred outcomes and instrumentalities are oriented toward control, supervision, limitation, and education for self-restraint in sexual behavior outside marriage.

The agency, an instrument of the Jewish community whose mission is to provide social services to a broad spectrum of Jews, is placed in a delicate position. As a social service agency, it is guided by professional social work values; as a Jewish agency, it is committed to uphold Jewish values which may contradict social work values. The agency's conflict begins at the first level—preferred conceptions of people—and proceeds to the level of preferred outcomes and instrumentalities.

The path to resolving this conflict is at the level of conception, where the conflict originated, not on the level of practice. Thus, the agency's administration needs to engage in dialogue with the other parties on their respective conceptions of the client. For this dialogue, information on the capabilities, differential behaviors, and varying degrees of responsibility of individuals with cognitive disabilities needs to be made available. Such knowledge can influence the values and opinions of the parties involved.

Social workers maintain that a diagnosis of cognitive disability, in and of itself, should not limit a person's right to sexual self-expression. The agency's responsibility, from a social work perspective, is to assist individuals in developing relationships and to provide concerned parties with information about cognitive disability as it pertains to sexuality. This information provides a basis for making sound policy decisions and accepting responsibility for such decisions.

The Orthodox Jewish community insists that the value of abstinence should take precedence over information and knowledge about capacity for self-expression. From a Judaic perspective, sexuality is an expression of the marital relationship, not of chance encounters.

Although information about the social behavior of individuals with mental handicaps may illuminate the conflict, concerned parties need to confront one another at the level of values.

THE AGENCY'S DILEMMA

The agency faces the dilemma of having all three parties to the conflict among its constituencies. The social workers on staff, the parents of the clients, and the Jewish community that sponsors and supports the agency represent differing value orientations with regard to the client group. However, in addition to this value conflict, the various parties have different notions of the agency's mission within the community.

For the social work staff, the agency's primary mission is to service the needs of individuals and families in a professional manner, guided by the values and ethics of the social work profession. Although religious needs are incorporated into treatment as they become manifest, the client's "Jewishness" is not the primary concern. Rather, the practitioner's primary concern is the individual's fit and interaction with the social environment.

For the parents, the agency serves as the caretaker for their children. As such, it should provide a safe and supervised environment where their children's basic needs are met. The agency is perceived as an agent of social control established by the community for people who cannot live independently and need supervision. In addition to providing basic care, the agency is expected to set limits on acting-out behavior. Sexual intercourse is an example of such behavior and is not acceptable to parents.

The Jewish community views the agency as an instrument of Jewish continuity. The raison d'etre of Jewish Family Services is to perpetuate Jewish communal life by strengthening the Jewish family and enabling Jewish individuals to lead more productive lives. Its primary mission is directed toward the survival of the Jewish group. As such, the agency should uphold Jewish values.

The dilemma is aggravated by Maryland's expectation that the agency conform to its rules and regulations, which guarantee persons with mental disability the right to sexual self-expression.

CONCLUSIONS

The agency's board of directors approved the following policy (Howard et al. 1991, p. 364):

- Staff will provide sexuality counseling, guidance, and education, as necessary and appropriate.
- Sexual expression will be permitted—or restricted—on an individual basis, as determined jointly by the professional and the client, and based on the needs, desires, value orientation, and capabilities of the resident(s). Potential consequences, including the impact on the privacy of others, will be carefully considered.
- Sexual intercourse is not permitted on JFS property between nonmarried adults.

This policy represents a compromise between professional values, government regulations, and Jewish values. The compromise process involved numerous meetings and deliberations among various agency constituents. Deliberations began in the agency's ethics committee. Staff defined and analyzed the value stances of the parties: clients, board, Judaism, government, parents, community, professionals, agency. The ethics committee consulted with experts on government regulations and an Orthodox rabbi. Jewish agencies with residential services were surveyed. The author was invited to help the staff think through the value issues. The board of directors, rabbis, and staff were consulted and given opportunities for input.

The Orthodox community was intimately involved in the policy-making process. In Baltimore, Orthodox Jews constitute 20 percent of the Jewish population (compared with 6.8 percent of all Jews across the United States). They are a dominant force in the local Jewish community and are represented on the boards of the Jewish agencies. Though a minority, they are a vocal group who want the agency to adhere to its Jewish character by recognizing the primacy of religious law in agency policies. However, other religious groups in the Jewish community have less stringent standards. Jewish Family Services must balance these conflicting demands because its mission is to serve the entire Jewish community. In this case, particular sensitivity to the Orthodox view was considered necessary.

In developing the agency's policy, parents did not directly participate in the decision-making process. Jewish Family Services made assumptions about what their views would be, based on its experience with parents of adults with cognitive disabilities. After the adoption of the policy, parents are given information during intake about agency philosophy, programs, and services, including the policy on sexual behavior. They then have the opportunity to question and explore the implications of the policy for their son or daughter.

Anticipating that clients may violate the policy in the course of exercising their self-determination (i.e., having sexual intercourse on agency property), Jewish Family Services attempts to prevent violations by preparing clients as well as possible. During the intake process, potential clients are informed of this policy and are afforded the option of choosing another agency if the policy conflicts with their preferred life-style. In implementing the policy, the agency takes precautions not to unduly restrict sexual expression that is consensual, legal, and not socially stigmatizing. Although the residences have varying degrees of supervision, some residents are left on their own at times in an effort to promote independence.

If clients violate the policy, the staff help them to explore other options for sexual expression that are consistent with the policy, assisting them to the fullest extent possible to develop options that will allow them to remain in the program. To date, no client with mental disability has been forced to make the choice between remaining in a residential program and exercising his or her right to sexual expression.

The compromise was viewed by many as inadequate. Neither side won, but neither side lost. The Orthodox community, though unhappy about the extent to which independent discretion is permitted, recognized that the agency had attempted to address their views in the policy. The staff questioned whether the policy fully respects the clients' rights to self-determination.

By permitting some sexual contacts and prohibiting others, Jewish Family Services demonstrated its ability to reconcile fundamental value conflicts at the practice, or instrumental, level. The conflict on the level of preferred conceptions has not been resolved. Significant divisions among the parties still remain on how they prefer to view cognitively handicapped persons. The agency is still grappling with the complex issues that have been raised. "This policy does not end the debate; it simply helps to define it. It sets guidelines and minimal expectations for the delicate balancing act required of both board and staff" (Howard et al. 1991, p. 365).

Is the policy ethical? Since ethics are based on values that reflect general moral standards, an action is deemed to be ethical if it is consistent with the value. Permission to express oneself sexually is based on the values of human dignity, self-determination, and personal fulfillment. The prohibition against engaging in sexual intercourse is based on the Jewish value of abstinence before marriage. The agency, guided by professional values and Jewish values, has opted to reflect both value systems in the compromise decision. The policy is, therefore, ethical.

As a result of this process, the agency has taken several steps to reorient its various constituents toward redefining their preferred conceptions of individuals with mental retardation. Constituents include the Jewish community, parents, and professional staff. The agency's coordinator of residential services for adults with developmental disabilities published an article in the *Baltimore Jew-*

ish Times, a weekly newspaper widely read by persons from the various religious segments in the Jewish community. The author pointed out the need to view people with disabilities as human beings first. "When we use people-first language, words that emphasize the person first and the disability second, we affirm the humanity of those with disabilities and emphasize ways in which they are similar to us" (Howard et al. 1992). In addition, the agency has offered a Jewish Family Life Workshop for parents of adults with disabilities, in which participants learn about trends in services and resources and explore such issues as sexuality, relationships, and involvement in the community.

Staff has maintained a dialogue with parents regarding religious and nonreligious issues. New direct-service staff participate in a three-hour module on human rights concerning the right to privacy and dignity. Staff also receive training on the sexuality of people with disabilities at the Kennedy-Krieger Institute of Johns Hopkins Hospital.

The community needs to be educated about the preferred conceptions of people with disabilities in order to reorient its thinking, values, and policies. Parents, too, need information regarding the potential of their disabled children. Staff need to be trained in the capacities, limitations, values, and ethical issues regarding people with disabilities. All of us are enriched by the full citizenship and participation of people with differing abilities, perspectives, and contributions.

Professionals in Jewish communal service can learn from this process of decision-making and value analysis. Among the three types of decision-making—domination, compromise, and creative alternatives—the JFS decision seems to have achieved the highest classification. By adopting a policy of creative alternatives, Jewish Family Services of Baltimore was able to defuse an explosive situation and conform to ethical standards.

By adopting the values classification model, professionals have a tool with which to analyze conflicting positions in policy-making and service provision. The key to this approach is to begin the analysis with preferred conceptions of the client, where the source of the conflict may lie. Discussion proceeds to preferred outcomes, but ultimately focuses on instrumentalities, the values of direct practice, where creative alternatives can be explored.

Chapter 5

Value Conflicts in Nursing Home Placement

This chapter delineates the value conflicts and process of decision-making in placing an elderly couple in a nursing home. The central theme is about choice: how one goes about choosing to perform a particular act in an ethically ambiguous situation. The choice is difficult to make, and it is usually the result of an intellectual and emotional struggle. Intellectually, knowledge of the facts can sometimes lead to one action, but if the facts change, they can lead to the opposite action. Emotionally, there are times when the values on both sides of the case can be strongly supported, which makes it difficult for the professional to make the "right" choice.

One of the ways of reducing options is to resort to principles. As guides to action, principles offer external imperatives that command and justify particular actions in specific circumstances. The struggle to choose is thereby alleviated, but so is the creativity inherent in the process of choosing. According to Neuborne (1987), Judge Bork, who was nominated and rejected for the United States Supreme Court, was guilty of this pattern.

> He is incapable of performing the most important task we set before our Supreme Court Justices: forging a personal vision of the Constitution from the raw material of text, history, tradition, precedent, logic, experience and heart. . . . Judge Bork refuses to accept the burden of choice [because he seeks] an external source of command that relieves him of the responsibility of choice.

In choosing between one ethical action and another, the individual is usually faced with the burden of choosing between two "rights" and two "goods" that possess equal weight and importance. Then one must resort to values and knowledge, "history, tradition, precedent, logic, experience and heart." The process of making ethical choices will be demonstrated through the value analysis that was presented in chapter 1 and is now applied to a case of nursing home placement.

AN ETHICAL DILEMMA

The following dilemma was presented by the staff of a Jewish Family Service:

> Mr. and Mrs. W. have severe physical disabilities that put them at risk. Both need nursing home placement or chronic hospitalization. They refuse, and are adamant about remaining in their own home. Despite the fact that Jewish Family Service is providing as much support as its resources will allow, the couple still remain at risk. There is no extended family which can be relied upon. The community is aware of their plight and is concerned about their welfare.
>
> Do we have a right to tell this couple that we will withdraw our services after a time-limited period in the hope that this might move them into accepting the institutional plan they so desperately need?

The paradigm to be applied here, set forth in table 5, differs from the one discussed in the preceding chapter. In that situation, the values of the three parties to the conflict served to justify their policy stances on the clients' sexual behavior, so the clients' values were not included. In this case, a different paradigm is used to depict the interrelated values, practice, and ethics of each of the parties. This paradigm, not limited to a value analysis but including action and ethics, offers an additional model of analysis.

Values commit individuals and groups to action. Ethics is values in action. In discerning the values of each of the parties in this situation, the appropriate action and ethics would be determined.

VALUES

The couple's values are to retain their independence and remain at home with its attendant security, familiarity, and feeling of

Table 5: A Values–Practice–Ethics Paradigm

Couple	Professional	Agency	Community
Values Home-security, familiarity, belonging; self-determination	Client self-determination; preserving life and the quality of life; equitable distribution of resources	Preserving life and the quality of life; just equitable distribution of resources; community sanction	Protection of couple; living up to community's social norms
Practice Remain at home; agency continue support services	Offer choice and abide by couple's decision; refer to protective service agency or to home for the aged	Refer to agency protective placement service or home for the aged	
Ethics Yes	Yes on both	Yes	Yes

belonging. They express these wishes to the agency, and thus far have been able to withstand the pressure to leave their home for a nursing home.

The professional subscribes to two contradictory values. She believes in the client's right to self-determination, but also in preserving life and a quality of life that is perhaps equal to, or surpasses, the value of self-determination. Since it has been determined that the couple's well-being is at risk, the value of preserving life would seem to take precedence. Yet, the couple have been subsisting in their home with the agency's assistance. This testifies to their ability to make it on their own. The capacity for self-determination and for living in one's home are formidable values that need to be supported, but so is the value of preserving life.

A third professional value that derives from the professional's administrative role is the agency's equitable distribution of limited resources to benefit the maximum number of people. Available information suggests that the couple would require additional funds as their physical condition deteriorates, thus making these funds unavailable to others.

Related to this value is the agency's fiscal stability. In many states, decisions toward institutionalization of the elderly are driven by reimbursement policies which tend to be in-patient oriented. If the agency stands to be better reimbursed when it institutionalizes a client, the decision-making process inclines in that direction. This issue was not raised during the deliberation.

The value of client self-determination is a professional value, not an agency value. The agency values protection of the lives of the clients who are under its jurisdiction. The agency also values justice and the equitable distribution of resources to reach as many needy people as possible.

A third agency value is Jewish community sanction. Supported by community funds and guided by community leaders, the agency feels duty bound to reflect and implement Jewish communal values and norms in its policies and services. The dominant Jewish value in this case is the preservation of life. It is the community's responsibility to preserve the life of its members, even as it is the individual's own responsibility.

Even if this value were not clearly articulated by the community, the professional staff would still be responsible for influencing the laity and community about the supreme value of the preservation of life, as well as other values it deems important. For the professional's role is not only to reflect community values, but to educate the community in value enunciation and implementation.

The community wants the couple to be protected from physical debilitation. It also expects its members to live up to certain social norms, such as maintaining a clean and well-kept house. It is widely known that the couple are unable to do this due to their deteriorating health. The community's values show concern for the couple's well-being and for the maintenance of community norms.

PRACTICE AND ETHICS

In respecting the couple's values, the professional affirms their wish to remain at home and continues to provide support services. This is the ethical thing to do because it is consistent with the couple's values and with professional values. It is "good" from a utilitarian perspective because it leads to good outcomes: it preserves their independence, mental health, and feelings of security and belonging. It also maintains their identity by providing sameness and continuity in living arrangements.

The professional, though, is faced with a practice problem and an ethical dilemma because she subscribes to conflicting values. Supporting the client's right to self-determination should commit the professional to give the couple a choice between remaining in their home and entering a nursing home. If the couple choose to stay, the professional is ethically bound to honor this decision because it is consistent with the professional value of client self-determination.

The professional also values the preservation and quality of life. She could refer the couple to the protective-services agency, suggest institutional placement, or provide 24-hour care. These options are based on her knowledge, supported by medical data, that the couple's physical condition has deteriorated, their lives are in danger, and they need a total protective environment. Their wish to remain at home would be overridden.

All three of these practice options are ethically appropriate because they are based on the professional value of preserving life and the quality of life. The professional would, therefore, be ethically bound to investigate each option and then determine their order of priority.

As an administrator, the professional's value of justice would require the agency not to increase the funds for this couple. The agency should continue to provide financial support at the current level, but if more is needed, the agency need not expend it, for there may not be enough for the equitable distribution of scarce resources to other clients. This decision is ethical because it is consistent with the agency's equitable-distribution value. This value takes into account the agency's concern for the needs of other clients and legitimate concern for its own fiscal viability.

Hence it would be ethical for the professional to convey to the couple the limits of the agency's financial commitment to maintain them at home.

The professional's values of preservation of life and equal distribution of resources coincide with the agency's values. It would, therefore, be ethical for the agency to refer the couple for protective services or a home for the aged, and to limit its financial outlay to them.

The community's values include the couple's protection and their living up to communal norms by maintaining a well-kept house. The neighbors are aware of the couple's physical disabilities and want them placed in a protective environment where their physical needs will be met. Not permitting the neglect of their house will also have the effect of curbing the deterioration of the neighborhood.

The plan of action is ethical, for it is consistent with the community's values, which are dual in nature: preserving the couple's life and the community's aesthetic appearance.

CONFLICTS AMONG PARTIES

The four parties in this case are in conflict with each other. On the extremes, the couple want to remain at home, and the agency and community want them institutionalized. The professional is caught in the middle because her values lean toward the couple's and also toward the agency's and community's. She is faced with an ethical dilemma because she espouses conflicting values. The value of self-determination requires the professional to offer the couple the choice of remaining at home. The value of protection of life requires her to encourage other resolutions of the problem besides remaining at home. The value of justice—the equitable distribution of resources—requires the professional and the agency to limit the expenditure of funds and not increase or reduce its allocation.

Since each of these options is based on a legitimate professional value, the adoption of any one of them would be considered ethical. One way of proceeding to answer the question of what is the right and good thing to do is to anticipate the consequences of each action. As Lewis (1984) states, it is conceivable that the more knowledge that is brought to bear in an ethically ambiguous situation, the greater the possibility of clarifying the options and ultimately choosing the one most appropriate.

If the professional acts on the value of self-determination and gives the couple the choice, they will most likely decide to remain at home. If the professional acts on the value of preservation of life, she will make a referral to the protective agency or to an institution. Since the option of 24-hour care directly contradicts the equitable distribution of resources value, it is not a viable consideration.

If the professional, as an administrator, acts on the value of justice, she conveys to the couple the limits of agency funding. The couple still has the choice of determining where they want to live, but they are now better informed of the agency's service parameters. There is, then, a conflict between two professional values— self-determination and preservation of life. This leads to the ethical dilemma.

MAKING THE ETHICAL CHOICE

The conflict between self-determination and preservation of life may not be irreconcilable if they are viewed as progressive values: a value that is dominant at one time may be superseded by another value at another time. In this case, while the couple are still able to hold their own with limited agency assistance, the value of self-determination may be more dominant than any other value. As their health deteriorates, however, the value of protection may become more dominant and supersede the value of self-determination. If medical knowledge attests to their increasing deterioration, it supports the professional's preference for protection over self-determination.

Moreover, self-determination may be considered an active value only if the couple are capable of weighing the consequences of their decision rationally. It is conceivable that they may be deemed incapable due to their deteriorating health. In this scenario, the professional will make the decision, because capacity is judged by others. They decide whether paternalism is called for, or whether a person shall be allowed to rule his own life. Chachkes (1988) contends that professionals have a responsibility to protect clients who cannot protect themselves. When the right to protection conflicts with the right to self-determination, the professional may deem the latter to take second place to the former. Though this decision may evoke paternalistic concerns, it introduces professional responsibility into the client's exercise of autonomy. The challenge for professionals is to meet their responsibilities in the least restrictive way.

The progression of values and the knowledge of changing circumstances seem to support Lewis's contention that "an approach that depends on an evaluation of consequences is likely to yield a tentative choice of action, subject to revisions or modification during the entire service transaction, constantly responding to new data generated by the service process itself" (Lewis 1984, p. 208). As new information becomes available from physicians' testimony regarding the couple's physical condition, the utilitarian approach may advocate a shift from respecting the couple's right to remain at home to assuming a more protective role. The theory might support the principle of nonmaleficence—do no harm—which could justify the rule that people who cannot take care of themselves should be protected by the community. In the absence of such information regarding their physical debility, the mandate may not be as clear.

This approach might have served as the rationale behind the agency's question when it posed the ethical dilemma: "Do we have a right to tell this couple that we will withdraw our services after a time-limited period in the hope that this might move them into accepting the institutional plan they so desperately need?" In the agency's judgment, the threat to withdraw services is designed to achieve a greater good: better care and protection in a nursing home. The agency is asking whether the value of protection should supersede the value of self-determination.

If the professional and the agency were to subscribe to deontological theory as supportive of principles, they might have a clearer mandate for action. This theory reasons from general ethical imperatives, or prima facie duties that are deemed to be self-evident in the situation. In this case, the principle of respect for the couple's autonomy is equivalent to the principle and prima facie duty of beneficence (Ross 1930). The responsibility to protect the couple's health and life stems from the principle and prima facie duty of nonmaleficence. The duty to prevent harm, according to Ross, takes priority over other prima facie duties. It is self-evident that protection of life is a greater duty than respecting autonomy.

In discussing the options of placing an elderly man in a nursing home based on formalist (deontological) and consequentialist (utilitarian) theories, Lewis offers numerous possibilities that are determined by consequences. If the consequences are not life-threatening, Lewis advises following the formalist approach—i.e., respecting the man's autonomy. If they are life-threatening, the greater good is to place the individual in a nursing home. Where there is ambiguity, the choice may be either to respect autonomy or to place in an institution (Lewis 1984).

It is apparent that a theory cannot tell the practitioner what to do in an ethically ambiguous situation. It can frame the question and provide the context for the principles, values, and knowledge. The resolution of the dilemma is not to be found in the objective situation, which can have different interpretations, but in the professional's weighing of principles and values. Once the decision is made, the professional should be able to legitimate it based on knowledge, values, principles, and theory, and not merely on instinct or feeling.

Since theory cannot prescribe, it requires principles to guide practitioners in ethically ambiguous situations. Loewenberg and Dolgoff (1992, p. 60) offer an Ethical Principles Screen of priorities in ethical decision-making.

Ethical Principles Screen
Ethical Principle 1. Principle of protection of life
Ethical Principle 2. Principle of equality and inequality
Ethical Principle 3. Principle of autonomy and freedom
Ethical Principle 4. Principle of least harm
Ethical Principle 5. Principle of quality of life
Ethical Principle 6. Principle of privacy and confidentiality
Ethical Principle 7. Principle of truthfulness and full disclosure

This screen can serve as an objective guideline for practitioners who may be unable to decide between competing principles. It is a useful, but not absolute, index of priorities. Even Ethical

Principle 1—the protection of life—which is the supreme value, may not be a priority when the threat to life is ambiguous. Practitioners should have the freedom to rearrange these priorities if, in their judgment, the situation warrants it.

RESOLVING THE DILEMMA

The agency had asked whether it was ethical to remove the service in order to force the couple to enter a nursing home. From the perspective of deontological theory, the prima facie duty of fidelity requires that a person keep a promise out of loyalty to the other person. Having already put the service in place, the agency had, in effect, made a promise to the couple to support them in their home. In medical ethics, it is deemed unethical to remove life-sustaining treatments to sick people once they are in place. Here, too, it would be unethical to remove "life-sustaining" services to the couple. This decision, however, did not imply that the agency supported the couple's autonomy. It merely opposed the agency's intention to remove the services.

The agency was seeking ways to encourage the couple to enter a nursing home, and the couple did go. The dilemma was resolved when the agency decided that, based on the knowledge that their physical condition was deteriorating, it was more important to try to preserve the couple's lives than to respect their wish to stay at home.

CONCLUSION

A process of thinking about ethics and ethical dilemmas has been presented. The professional does not decide impulsively how to act in an ethically ambiguous situation but thinks through the alternatives. The decision, a product of sound professional judgment, must be based on professional values and ethical principles. Ethical dilemmas can usually be resolved in either direction because both alternatives are right and good. The soundness of the decision is determined by the gathering of as much knowledge of the situation as possible, the delineation and ordering of the values of each party to the conflict, and the application of ethical principles supported by theories. An Ethical Principles Screen offers an objective set of priorities in ethical decision-making.

Chapter 6

Personal Values vs. Professional Values

Conflicts between personal and professional values invariably confront professional practitioners in the course of their daily work. A difference in race, class, religion, or ethnic group can underscore a difference in values. When the professional's values are deeply ingrained, especially from religious sources, there is a strong impulse to prevent the client from violating religious norms. One needs to be especially on guard to prevent their intrusion into the professional relationship.

What is the professional to do with personal values: are they to be repressed or expressed? Levy (1976*b*, p. 119) suggests that the professional need not be prevented from representing or enunciating personal values. There are times when the professional's personal values represent a practical and useful alternative for clients, especially if they fulfill clients' needs.

> But representing personal values as an alternative is different from insisting upon them as a preference, simply because they are a preference for the practitioner. The question the practitioner must ask of himself is whether he is offering his client an alternative to consider in the light of his needs, or a bias to which his client must conform on pain of negative judgment or the deprivation of service.

Personal values need not be repressed, but merely constrained toward meeting client needs rather than personal needs.

Loewenberg and Dolgoff (1992) argue with Levy's contention (1976*b*, p. 113) that "To be a professional practitioner is to give up one's autonomy and to relinquish some of one's rights as a freely functioning being." They understand this to mean that professionals must suspend or neutralize all personal values when serving clients. Levy actually meant that the practitioner may not give full expression to personal values just because they are important to the professional; they are to be used in the service of the client. The professional needs to have a full understanding of values and biases, deal with clients where they are, and help them understand the consequences of their options. Personal values may not be imposed, but they can be used in the service of clients.

The three cases that follow reflect different aspects of the personal-professional values conflict. The first involves a long-standing personal relationship that clashes with the professional function. The second involves personal relationships that prevent the fulfillment of administrative responsibilities. The third involves the conflict of religious values with professional values.

MY FRIEND, THE EXECUTIVE DIRECTOR

A committee that I staff at federation has decided not to continue funding a specific program at a certain agency. The information is available to me, but I may not share it with my long-time friend who is the executive director of the agency. The committee's policy is that decisions in the midst of the budgeting process may not be revealed because changes may still be made. This restriction weighs heavily on me because my dearest friend, who was there for me then I went through crises in my life, will be negatively impacted by the decision when he finds out three months from now. There will be less time for everyone affected to make alternate plans. Early warning should be given to teachers who may have to be laid off, and to working parents who will need to find alternative placements for their children. I know in my heart that I should really share the information with him, and yet I feel a responsibility to the committee.

This is an ethical dilemma because I feel that I am being dishonest in our personal relationship. I have information in my hand that he should have and I cannot give it to him because I was asked not to. It's frustrating.

There is an unwritten contract with my lay committee that what transpires at meetings will be kept confidential. My own ethical system also says that I really should not be sharing the information. What creates the dilemma is not the withholding but the consequences of withholding. I believe that the people being served should have the information so they can plan their lives.

Resolution. I could suggest to the agency executive that he prepare for some cuts in the programs. But if he asks me to provide more details, I will have to refuse. I made a decision not to do what I really want to do, and I agonize over it.

Discussion

The conflict between the professional's personal and professional relationship with the executive director is located in the tension between friendship and confidentiality. Maintaining the friend's trust necessitates the violation of confidentiality. Keeping confidentiality adversely affects the friend, the agency's staff, and the people served.

Maintaining the friendship is supported by the prima facie duties of fidelity and gratitude, which impel the professional to share the information with the executive. These duties are buttressed by the ethical principles of beneficence and nonmaleficence, which require the professional to enable the clients to plan their next steps. The principles guide the professional to serve people in the least harmful manner. The professional would, therefore, be acting ethically by informing the executive of the committee's decision because it adversely affects services to the members of the agency. However, short of revealing the committee's decision, the professional still has an ethical duty to assure an adequate time warning and to confront the committee with the implications of not warning.

On the other side, there are good reasons for not divulging the committee's decision. It may change, and this may bring other consequences in its wake. Previous experiences confirm that leaks in budgetary decisions usually come back to haunt the decision-makers and the professional staff, especially when they have a negative impact on the agency. The committee's insistence on confidentiality is intended to avoid these negative consequences. The same principle of nonmaleficence that supports revealing the committee's decision can also support the maintenance of confidentiality in order to avoid causing harm.

The professional has opted to abide by the committee's policy on confidentiality but has found a way to warn his friend about forthcoming cuts that do not violate the policy. Confidentiality is preserved when the duty of fidelity to the committee's authority to make its governing rules is carried out. Though some harm may ensue by not revealing the information at this time, the harm is inevitable when the cuts are announced. There is a net gain of promoting good over harm by preserving confidentiality.

This decision was fraught with the moral anguish of an option not taken, of the hurt inflicted on a friend. It left moral traces that were not easily forgotten.

RETRENCHING PERSONAL FRIENDS

There are two unproductive administrators who have been here a very long time, are near retirement, and are ill. Neither of them needs the job for financial security. One is a close personal friend and the other is someone of whom I am very fond. They have stood by me through personal and professional crises in this agency.

I have been asked to dismiss these people, as the agency is in a period of retrenchment. This could possibly save the jobs of four of the bright, newer workers whom we want to keep. We have a dossier of their wrongdoings that gives evidence of their incompetence. But I cannot do it, even though I know that it would be best for the agency if they retired.

Resolution. I have tried to get a postponement for several months, citing their progressive illnesses, the pending marriage of a daughter, their desire to retire on their own, and the presence of other inefficient staff on payroll.

Discussion

This case is similar to the previous one in that the professional needs to overcome the feeling of hurting friends in the course of performing a professional duty. It is always difficult to fire staff, but especially when one has had a close relationship with them. The professional is expected to place professional duty before friendship, which is facilitated due to the staff's incompetence.

The two cases are similar in the nature of the conflict and its ethical imperatives. In the first case, the friendship creates a conflict between preserving and violating confidentiality. The ethical imperative is to preserve confidentiality, though the friend will be hurt. Here, the friendship poses a conflict between retaining and releasing incompetent staff. The ethical imperative is to dismiss the staff, though they will be hurt. The professional has little discretion in the matter.

The conflict in this case is between fidelity to long-standing friendships, and fidelity to agency continuity in a time of retrenchment. The professional knows that dismissing the staff members will redound to the greater good of the agency. It will permit the retention of younger, more able staff and provide better service to clients. The principles of utility, fidelity, and beneficence justify the decision to terminate their employment.

Yet, the professional cannot bring herself to carry out the task. Deep feelings of friendship—fidelity—interfered with her professional function and evoked the anguish of violating her professional responsibility. Though she argued that staff near retirement who are psychologically most vulnerable should be permitted to terminate gracefully, her action was unethical.

RELIGIOUS VALUES AND PROFESSIONAL VALUES

A social worker in a Jewish family agency describes her ethical dilemma with a Jewish family.

> I am working with a family consisting of parents in their thirties and a seven-year-old child. The father, a recovering drug addict, has been drug-free for about four years in response to his wife's threat to divorce him if he does not abandon drugs. About a year ago he joined Jews for Jesus because the group accepted him as an addict and persuaded him that Jesus is a forgiving God, in contrast to the Jewish God.
>
> Friction in the family has increased because the husband wants his wife to go to church and eventually convert. The child had attended a yeshiva but was removed and placed in public school. Due to his mother's insistence that he attend Sunday school to learn Hebrew, he now attends Sunday school.

Personally, I am having a very hard time with this family conflict. I come from Russia, where many people left Judaism, but my parents instilled religion and Godliness in me, and I had to struggle to maintain my Jewishness.

I am very angry with the husband and am trying not to bring my countertransference into the session. I work mostly with the wife and support her as much as I can, but occasionally I see them as a couple. The child is conflicted; he goes to Hebrew school on Sundays but is also taken to church occasionally by his father.

As a professional, I know I have to separate my own feelings and start where the family is at, but I am in conflict between my professionalism and my feelings. I take some of the credit for his being drug-free, so it is frustrating that he is doing something that really hurts me. He joined Jews for Jesus while I was working with his wife, and I am partially blaming myself.

Resolution. The wife has low self-esteem, is passive, and not prone to express anger. But she communicated her anger and rage to her husband. This represents great progress for her. Therapy has helped her to think more clearly and verbalize her wants.

I explored my client's feelings about God and about the higher power, which is very popular in the twelve-step program. She liked the idea of presenting my suggestion to her husband, that they agree that there is one God, refrain for the time being from naming the God and just call Him God. The husband has agreed not to mention Jesus, but to use phrases such as "with God's help" in order not to confuse the child. It was this compromise that resolved my personal/professional conflict and eased the tension between them.

To be sure, all the tensions have not disappeared. There persist the husband's addictive personality (his alcoholism, cult-orientation), the disagreements about raising the child, religious practices in the home, etc. But the sore point about substituting Jesus for God has been temporarily assuaged.

Discussion

The professional's conflict is between her personal values, which were influenced by her Jewish background, and her professional values, which are directed toward meeting client needs. As a Jew born in atheistic Russia whose Jewishness was maintained against all odds, she cannot brook American Jews who relinquish their Jewishness for another religion. She believes that Jewishness is a precious gift and cannot understand why anyone would want to discard it. She is so deeply steeped in her Jewish identity that she wants to prevent others from escaping from theirs. She is, therefore, opposed to this family's becoming involved in Jews for Jesus and the child becoming religiously and psychologically damaged.

As a professional, the social worker is guided by the principle of client self-determination. Her professional role is to help the family decide what it wants to do and what the possible consequences might be. This family is religiously split. The husband has joined a Christian cult and the wife wants to preserve the family's Jewish identity by providing a Jewish education for their son.

What ought the social worker to do? Should she go along with the husband's inclination to adopt Christianity as the family religion, or build up the wife's self-esteem to oppose her husband? The wife is the primary client; the husband, only occasionally. The wife wants to retain the family's Jewish identity. In order to effect this goal, she needs to be able to stand up to her husband and express her difference. The social worker opted to support the wife's self-determination.

Supporting the wife's self-determination coincided with the social worker's personal values regarding the preservation of Jewish identity. Her personal values were not offered as an alternative to the client's values, nor as a bias to which the client was expected to conform (Levy 1976b). This is alluded to in the social worker's control of her countertransference. She used her values to reinforce the client's emotional identification with the Jewish community and to suggest a compromise with the husband. By agreeing to drop the name of Jesus and substitute the name of God, the husband reduced tensions in the family.

CONCLUSION

The three cases reflect different conflicts between personal values and professional values. In the first case, the professional opted to support the value of confidentiality, though he hurt his friend in the process by not revealing the committee's decision. In the second, the professional was not able to override her friendship with two employees by performing the professional task of dismissal. In case three, the professional was able to utilize her personal values in the service of the client.

In the conflict between personal values and professional values, the professional is duty-bound to uphold professional values. Personal values need not be repressed, but can serve as an alternative or in support of the client's inclination. In cases where personal values are overridden (the first case), or where they should be (the second), the professional feels moral anguish over the choice not made. Though the pain lingers, it is assuaged by the knowledge that correct ethical action has been taken.

Chapter 7

Professional and Personal Priorities

This chapter continues the theme of personal values vs. professional values, with the focus on setting priorities. Setting priorities in allocations, and between personal and professional obligations, involves the ordering of values. "Setting priorities is the hardest thing any community can do. There are as many definitions of what is important as there are constituencies in the Jewish communities, and as there are individual leaders representing those constituencies. A particular service may be very important to one group and unimportant to another" (Council of Jewish Federations 1991). Setting priorities is the knottiest of problems because competing claims on limited resources and on the use of time are based on deeply held values.

The Council of Jewish Federations (1991) assists federations to mobilize their communities to deal with priority setting by identifying issues and trends. No outsider can suggest to a community what its priorities should be. They vary from community to community, depending on the values of its leadership, and on economic and political realities.

This chapter suggests a Judaic perspective on professional and personal priorities in Jewish communal service. The major Judaic source of professional priorities can be found in the laws of *tzedakah*—social justice. Judaic sources on personal priorities derive from the high priest's animal sacrifices on Yom Kippur in the Temple, Moses' appointment of Joshua to succeed him as leader of the Jewish people, and a talmudic passage that poses a conflict between the demands of a mitzvah (commandment) and the demands of one's father. Personal and professional priorities are in the category of moral laws.

61

In Judaism, a distinction can be made between ritual and moral laws. Ritual laws are more precise. As an example, if sundown on Friday is at 5:32 p.m., then one minute before is still the weekday and one minute after is the Sabbath. There is a minute interval in which to desist from work, else one is guilty of violating the Sabbath.

Judaism is not as precise in the moral laws, which are addressed to interpersonal relationships. According to Rabbi Joseph B. Soloveitchik, the sages decided not to regulate such relationships in detail but to permit the parties to work them out themselves (Linzer 1978). This policy applies to laws of parent-child relationships and to *tzedakah*. The laws of *tzedakah* are central to an analysis of priority setting.

Conflicts with regard to priority setting in Jewish communal service exist on two levels: competing claims for funds to support agency services, and competing claims for the professional's time. This chapter is accordingly divided into two parts. The first discusses professional priorities in allocating scarce resources; the second, personal vs. professional priorities in discharging professional functions.

PROFESSIONAL PRIORITIES IN ALLOCATING SCARCE RESOURCES

The economic recession of the late 1980s and early 1990s, along with the curtailment of philanthropic giving by younger donors, has exacerbated the shortfall in communal fund-raising, causing many federations to reduce allocations to their constituent agencies. When there are insufficient resources to meet basic needs, on what basis should reductions be made? Should they be made across the board or differentially? How does one choose, for example, between Jewish education and transporting the elderly to the Y for a hot meal? Several scenarios are possible:

1. If funds are allocated to Jewish education and other services, transportation for the elderly will be eliminated.
2. If funds are allocated to Jewish education and other services, transportation for the elderly will be reduced.
3. Both scenarios in the reverse, with Jewish education as the dependent variable.

JUDAIC PERSPECTIVES

There are four conflict areas in which priorities need to be determined: (1) *pikuach nefesh* (preserving life); (2) the primacy of Torah study; (3) priorities in resource allocation; (4) responsibilities of recipients.

Pikuach Nefesh

The duty to preserve life is a supreme Jewish value. It is preferred over preserving the Sabbath and most of the other commandments.

> How do we know that the threat to life can supersede the Sabbath? Said R. Judah in the name of Samuel: "And you shall live by them" (Leviticus 18:5) and not die by them.
>
> (Talmud Yoma 85b)
>
> Regarding all the transgressions in the Torah, if some people say to an individual, "Transgress so that you will not be killed," let him transgress and not be killed, except for idolatry, immorality, and murder, as it is written: "And you shall live by them"—and not die by them.
>
> (Talmud Sanhedrin 74a)

According to the first selection, human life is supreme, for even the Sabbath, one of the holiest days of the year, could be superseded when human life is at stake. According to the second selection, while human life could override all the other precepts, three supersede it. The requirement to sacrifice one's life and not commit idolatry, adultery, or murder indicates that the preservation of human life is not an absolute value. There are values in Judaism for whose defense even life is sacrificed.

The three cardinal values supersede the preservation of life because they reflect the essence of the covenantal relationship between God and human beings. Idolatry represents the denial of God as the Supreme Being. Immorality is a threat to the family and the continuity of Jewish values. Murder is a violation of human sanctity.

There is no likelihood that priorities regarding the three cardinal sins will be invoked in federation work. Cases of *pikuach nefesh*—saving life—may be more applicable. How are we to understand *pikuach nefesh* in modern terms? Does it only apply if death may be imminent, such as a person suffering a heart attack, a terminal illness, a pregnant woman in the throes of labor pains, or does it also obtain when life is not in imminent danger, such as the elderly's need for nursing home care, drug addicts' need for rehabilitation, the homeless' need for shelter, shut-ins' need for food and companionship? If these needs also place individuals in the category of *pikuach nefesh,* should they precede allocations for "quality of life" type services, such as Jewish community centers, Jewish family services, intergroup relations, and camping? How broadly or narrowly should *pikuach nefesh* be defined? In addition, when *pikuach nefesh* situations clash with the need for Torah study—Jewish education—which takes precedence?

The Primacy of Torah Study

When compared with other positive mitzvot, Torah study takes precedence as it is more valued.

> These are the precepts which have no prescribed measure: the corner of a field [which must be left for the poor], the first-fruit offering, the pilgrimage, acts of kindness, and Torah study.
>
> (Mishnah Peah 1:1)

> These are the precepts whose fruits a person enjoys in this world but whose principal remains intact for him in the world to come. They are: the honor due to father and mother, acts of kindness, early attendance at the house of study morning and evening, hospitality to guests, visiting the sick, providing for a bride, escorting the dead, absorption in prayer, bringing peace between man and his fellow; and the study of Torah is equivalent to them all.
>
> (Talmud Shabbat 127a)

The text does not suggest ways to operationalize the primacy of Torah study. Primacy could refer to a preference for Torah study when it clashes with another mitzvah, or funding Jewish education before other services. The primacy of Torah study extends to Torah scholars.

> Our rabbis taught: He, his father, and his teacher [rabbi] were in captivity. He precedes his teacher [in being ransomed], his teacher precedes his father, his mother precedes them all. A scholar precedes a king of Israel because a dead scholar cannot be replaced, but a dead king can be replaced by any Jew.
>
> (Talmud Horayot 13a)

If his father and his teacher [rabbi] lost objects, his teacher's object should be returned first, for his father brought him into this world, but his teacher, who taught him Torah, brings him into the world to come.

(Talmud Baba Metzia 33a)

If there were many poor or captives before us and there was not enough money to support or clothe or redeem them all, the *kohen* [priest] precedes the *levi* [levite], the *levi* precedes the *yisrael* [ordinary Jew], etc. We follow this practice when their wisdom is on the same level, but if the *kohen gadol* [high priest] was uneducated and the *mamzer* [illegitimate son] was a Torah scholar, the Torah scholar comes first. Whoever possesses greater Torah scholarship precedes the other.

(Maimonides, Laws of Gifts to the Poor 8:17–18)

These passages reflect the Jewish preference for Torah study and for achieved status based on intellectual acumen over ascribed status. The uneducated high priest takes second place to the scholar who was born illegitimate. Jewish family lineage does not confer social status; intellectual achievement in Torah does.

The questions can now be joined. Which takes precedence: Torah study or *pikuach nefesh*? Is the paucity of Torah study a form of "spiritual suicide" for the Jewish people that ranks with threats to physical and mental well-being? Should the funding of Jewish education rank equally, take precedence, or be subordinate to the funding of *pikuach nefesh* services? How weighty is the potential spiritual suicide of the Jewish people when human lives are at stake? *Pikuach nefesh* services would appear to take precedence because of the duty to save physical life.

Priorities in the Allocation of Scarce Resources

The allocation of scarce resources is not a new problem. The sages of the Talmud were puzzled by the meaning of "sufficient" in the biblical command ". . . lend him sufficient for his need" (Deuteronomy 15:8). How much is sufficient? Their answer was formulated as a principle of *tzedakah:* "you are commanded to maintain him, but you are not commanded to make him rich" (Talmud Ketubot 67b). One must maintain the poor according to their previous life-style, but not excessively.

Guidelines for priorities may be inferred from this talmudic principle. "Maintenance" may be interpreted as supporting all existing services, even at a minimum. "Rich" may be interpreted as expanding services in a time of austerity. Though the new services are deemed to be necessary for an underserved population, the principle would caution agencies about supporting a policy of expansion in austere times. The moral obligation is to maintain existing services, and not to initiate new ones (Ribner 1991–92).

The talmudic principle, and the stories that follow it, is limited to individual Jews serving other individuals. It can be applied to agencies serving individuals but not to federations. Federations rarely have opportunities to discuss individual needs; they make their allocation decisions based upon agency needs. While federations help individuals through agencies, the line often undergoes significant filtering. Therefore, the talmudic principle directed toward individual needs should be seen in the context of the agency filter through which federations operate.

Responsibility of Recipients
Do recipients have any moral responsibility to curtail their requests in times of fiscal constraints? This question is discussed more fully in chapter 11 in connection with the resettlement of Jews from the former Soviet Union. In the story of Rabbi Nehemiah (Talmud Ketubot 67b), who offered lentils instead of fat chicken and old wine to a poor man from a good family and the man died, the onus was placed on the poor man, who should have reduced his expectations of the community's benefaction. The sages make the poor responsible for circumscribing their needs (Linzer 1990).

The talmudic principle may be applied to agencies. Agencies are exhorted to ask for less and reduce their "luxurious habits" when there are shortfalls in the campaign. While agency leaders may resent calling their "bread and butter" requests "luxurious habits," the story suggests that greater moral and fiscal responsibility must be taken for sustaining one's agency. Self-support is a Jewish ideal.

> A person should always push himself and even experience distress in order not to be dependent on others. He should not throw himself onto the community [to ask them to support him]. Our rabbis exhorted to make the Sabbath a weekday and not be dependent.

> Even if the person was an honored sage and became impoverished, let him get a menial, dishonorable job in order not to be dependent on others.
>
> (Maimonides, Laws of Gifts to the Poor 10:18)

In these days of fiscal constraints, self-support is not only an ideal but a pressing reality. Federations are allocating less resources to agencies, who need to achieve their budgetary goals through various fund-raising methods.

In sum, we have seen that in Judaism's lexical ordering of values, *pikuach nefesh,* Torah study, and Torah scholars are preeminent. Torah scholars take precedence in being accorded social honor due to their achievements in Torah learning.

Since *pikuach nefesh* supersedes Torah study and the Sabbath, can we assert that institutions that preserve physical life, such as hospitals and homes for the aged, should have funding priority over institutions concerned with quality of life, such as Jewish community centers, Jewish family services, college services, and camping? Jewish community centers claim to fulfill the goals of *pikuach nefesh* by offering a host of preventive services. These include nutrition counseling, exercise regimens, swimming classes, cardiac rehabilitation, and smoking-cessation classes. Should prevention be accorded priority over direct intervention in saving life? Perhaps not.

While it is clear that *pikuach nefesh* refers to physical health, can it be broadened to include mental health? Jewish family agencies promote both physical and mental health and prevent family dysfunction through nutrition programs, financial assistance and homelessness prevention, kosher food pantries, traditional counseling in cases of spouse and child abuse, suicidal ideation, single-parent families, the elderly, group homes, foster care, adoption, etc. If JCC and JFS services fall into the category of *pikuach nefesh* because they preserve physical and mental health, do they supersede scholarships for children who want to study Torah in a day school? Is prevention of ill health and family breakdown a greater priority than actual Torah study? The Talmud provides no objective guidelines in these conflict situations. They can only be answered by lay and professional leaders of agencies in conjunction with federations, guided by classical Judaic sources.

Summary

Pikuach nefesh, the primacy of Torah study, maintaining but not making the poor rich, are some of the conceptual tools provided by talmudic literature for determining priorities in the allocation of scarce resources. Because they are not as precise as the ritual laws and were formulated long ago, legitimate disagreements may occur on their application to contemporary federations and agencies.

Though the principle of maintaining individual poor persons is not applicable to federations, the overall moral principle of assisting the poor is an essential component of fund-raising campaigns. Most federations do not draw any lessons from Jewish teachings on priorities. They have carefully developed mission statements that are designed to drive the allocations and priority-setting processes. A direct linkage between allocations and Jewish thought is missing. Perhaps the link could be replaced through these concepts that provide a Jewish perspective on the complex subject of allocations and priority setting.

PERSONAL VS. PROFESSIONAL PRIORITIES IN DISCHARGING PROFESSIONAL FUNCTIONS

The second part of this chapter focuses on the dilemma of personal vs. professional priorities in discharging the professional function.

> One of the dilemmas I have is balancing my professional commitments with my family commitments. I am working in the federation because I want to make a contribution to Jewish life and to Jewish community. Yet I feel I undermine Jewish community on a personal level by not being there for my family when my children need me to help them with their homework, to give them breakfast, or to attend a play at school. It becomes increasingly difficult to balance my obligations to community and family, which are major values to me. I want to be able to do both. During the time that I am with my son at a baseball game or coaching his Little League, there are missed opportunities of soliciting people or developing new programs.

This is an example of a self-imposed dilemma. There are also examples of externally imposed dilemmas where a special meeting conflicts with a family commitment that had been set long before. Does Judaism have anything to say about these dilemmas? Since the value of community and the value of family are essential to the continuity of Jewish life, does one take priority over the other?

Three citations from classical Jewish tradition, respectively dealing with atonement, leadership, and parents, reflect the sages' approach to this dilemma.

On Yom Kippur, the high priest is told to atone "for himself, his household, and for the entire community of Israel" (Leviticus 16:17). In the process of atonement, family precedes community.

A second source highlights the tension between serving family and serving community. Before he dies, Moses suggests to God that a successor be appointed to lead the Israelites into the land of Israel (Numbers 27:17). God tells Moses to lay his hands upon Joshua and thereby transfer leadership to him.

Moses does not hint of his disappointment at not being allowed to continue leading the Israelites, nor does he nominate his sons to succeed him. His words reflect his concern for the welfare of his people. The sages, however, assumed that Moses did not lightly give up the idea of seeing his sons succeed him.

> "Let the Lord . . . set a man over the congregation" (Numbers 27:16). What prompted Moses to make this request immediately after the chapter dealing with the laws of inheritance? Since the daughters of Zelophehad inherited their father, Moses said: Now is the time to make my claims. If daughters inherit, then it is only right that my sons inherit my glory! Said the Holy One, blessed be He, to him: "Whoso keepeth the fig tree shall eat the fruit thereof" (Proverbs 27:18). Your sons idled away their time and did not occupy themselves with study of the Torah; but as for Joshua, much did he minister to you and much honor did he apportion to you. He would betake himself early in the morning and late in the evening to your meeting house, arranging the benches and spreading the mats. Since he served you with all his might, it is proper for him to minister to Israel, that he lose not his reward. "Take to thee Joshua the son of Nun"—in fulfillment of the text (Proverbs, loc. cit.): "Whoever keeps the fig tree, shall eat the fruit thereof."
>
> (Midrash Rabbah, Numbers 27:15–16)

Why did Moses' children idle away their time and not occupy themselves with Torah study? Perhaps Moses did not spend enough time with them, being so preoccupied with the community. He devoted his entire life to the community and was hardly ever at home. According to the sages, Moses did not resume normal marital life after the revelation at Sinai. He left his two sons on their own and did not pay special attention to them. Without the presence and guidance of their father, the sons spent their time in secular pursuits. In effect, the sages are blaming Moses for not functioning adequately as a father, and for placing indiscriminate priority on his communal obligations. Moses' children might have inherited his leadership had he taught them Torah and encouraged them to become involved in Jewish life. This incident prompted the sages to assert that parents are unable to bequeath Torah knowledge to children.

> Qualify yourself to study Torah, since it does not come to you by inheritance.
>
> (Pirke Avot 2:12)

> Why do not the children of scholars usually turn out to be scholars? Said Rabbi Yosef: That it should not be said that the Torah came to them by inheritance.
>
> (Talmud Nedarim 71a)

A third source of tension arises when simultaneous demands are made by one's father and a mitzvah. The child cannot do both at the same time. Whose honor comes first, one's father's or the mitzvah?

> Eleazar ben Mathia said: If my father orders me "Give me a drink of water" while I have a precept to perform, I disregard my father's honor and perform the precept, since both my father and I are bound to fulfill the precepts.
>   Issi ben Judah maintained: If the precept can be performed by others, it should be performed by others, while he should bestir himself for his father's honor.
>   Said Rabbi Mattena: The halakhah agrees with Issi b. Judah.
>
> (Talmud Kiddushin 32a)

The Talmud offers an approach to resolving conflicts of priorities. Though the fulfillment of a mitzvah is always a priority, it can be delegated to others so that the child's "personal" priority—fulfilling the father's request—may take precedence. Similarly in federation work, when a family commitment had been scheduled and a special committee meeting is called, the professional and lay leaders need to change the meeting date or to delegate another person to staff the meeting to enable the professional to meet family obligations. Reasonable people can work out agreeable solutions to these types of conflicts.

Summary

A pattern emerges in the three cases of atonement, leadership, and parents. When there is a conflict between personal/family and professional demands, the individual may not neglect family for exclusive devotion to community. Family may be a more important value than community, and commitments made to family need to be honored. When the individual is confronted with the dilemma of having to choose, the Talmud's resolution is to delegate another person to perform the mitzvah, staff the meeting, accomplish the task. Both tasks will then be done, and the individual will be free to fulfill the prior commitment to the family. Professionals who inevitably face a conflict between personal and professional priorities can be guided by principles from classical Jewish tradition.

CONCLUSION

This chapter completes the discussion of personal and professional values begun in the preceding chapter. Priority setting is a function of ordering among conflicting values, whether in the allocation process or in negotiating the demands of family and job. Judaic perspectives have illuminated the complex issues of priorities in Jewish communal service.

In the first section of the chapter, the principle of *pikuach nefesh* could not be directly applied to physical and mental health prevention services compared with direct threats to life and Torah study. The principle of "maintaining" and not making "rich" fell somewhat short in direct application to communal issues in social planning. However, these two principles provide a Judaic perspective and serve as a valuable tool for analysis. In the second section, the priority of family over community seemed to be more firm, especially when others could be delegated to handle the community obligation.

Chapter 8

The Ethics of Circumventing the Waiting List

Circumventing the waiting list is an ethical dilemma that frequently arises in some federation-affiliated agencies. The purpose of this chapter is to demonstrate various ways of thinking about ethics in order to provide professionals with some conceptual tools for analyzing ethical dilemmas.

ETHICAL DILEMMA

Two federation professionals describe their responses to an ethical dilemma that they frequently encounter:

Respondent I
One of the most serious dilemmas that I frequently confront arises when I get a call from an important rabbi who tells me that A has applied to the home for the aged where there is a waiting list. The person is very sick, lonely, perhaps doesn't have long to live, and the rabbi wants me to get her into the home, which may have a waiting list of 200 people. The ethical dilemma is, what is the right thing to do? Those on the waiting list are also needy. I have never been able to resolve it once and for all. Even though I feel very uncomfortable, there are times when I just try to push for this particular person. Sometimes it is a function of the caller's wealth and prestige in the community.

Respondent II

An area involving lay people is when they pressure you to get their relatives into a federation facility, such as a hospital or a home for the aged. My mother-in-law had applied for senior housing in the community in which we lived. Because there was a waiting list, she waited for three years before she got an apartment because I did not want to be seen as playing favorites.

Once I was pressured by the president of one of our agencies to get his brother into one of our homes for the aged. After doing some research, I discovered that his brother was not eligible for admission into that facility. I told the gentleman that his brother was not eligible. He cut his gift in half, and bought him a place in a private nursing home.

I try to act fairly and consistently in these kinds of matters by pointing out that when there are waiting lists, we try to abide by them.

The question may be asked as to whether this principle is absolute, or do I sometimes use discretion. Do I sometimes lean on people in order to influence them for somebody else? My answer is that sometimes I do. A colleague recently needed open-heart surgery. He wanted a private room in one of the federation hospitals. When I went to visit him, I saw that it was a very messy situation. I used my influence to get him the proper medical care and the admission to a private room. Sometimes I do use my influence to lean on people.

Discussion

While this dilemma may seem trivial compared to the issues confronting federations today, such as the need to strengthen Jewish identity and continuity, the shrinking government dollar, managed care, and the shortfall in the campaign, it provides an opportunity to conceptualize an ethical dilemma and the process for its resolution. Analysis proceeds along two dimensions: value conflict and ethical theory.

VALUE CONFLICT

Since ethics is based on values, an ethical dilemma presents a choice between two actions that are based on conflicting values. One approach to the analysis of this ethical dilemma is to study the underlying values of each action. The values can be classified into two groups: justice vs. fiscal adequacy, and preferred conceptions of clients as strangers vs. clients as intimates.

Justice vs. Fiscal Adequacy

Denial of the caller's request can be justified by upholding the value of justice. Acquiescence can be justified by commitment to the value of fiscal adequacy—the assurance of ample fiscal resources to meet community needs.

Federation operates on the value of justice, which includes such notions as fairness and fidelity, mutual respect and beneficence. According to Rawls (1981, p. 112),

> The main idea is that when a number of persons engage in a mutually advantageous cooperative venture according to rules, and thus restrict their liberty in ways necessary to yield advantages for all, those who have submitted to these restrictions have a right to a similar acquiescence on the part of those who have benefitted from their submission. We are not to gain from the cooperative labor of others without doing our fair share.

The waiting list is regulated by the principle of fairness—first come, first served. By agreeing to be placed on a waiting list, applicants restrict their freedom and must wait their turn for openings. They have a right to expect similar acquiescence on the part of the agency which has benefitted from their submission. The agency benefits by having a steady stream of clients available to fill beds. The agency's acquiescence is expressed in its agreement that, as openings occur, it will restrict intake to the waiting list. Outsiders who want to circumvent the waiting list are not to gain from the "cooperative labor of others without doing their fair share," which is to await their turn. Thus, the principle of fairness would deem political and economic pressure unethical because it violates the value of justice.

A contrary value is the fiscal viability of the agency. The donor with financial clout and leadership acumen contributes to the ongoing vitality of the agency. Such persons should not be alienated, lest they withdraw needed resources. The positive effect of coddling influential donors is the continuation of their financial support and leadership role in the agency. The negative effects are yielding to their power and influence and hesitating to criticize their actions when they appear to be wrong. Whether the professional's support for the lay person's actions is due to positive or negative factors, it reflects preference for the value of fiscal viability over the value of justice.

CLIENTS AS STRANGERS OR INTIMATES

Using Levy's classification of values (Levy 1973), we may begin with preferred conceptions of people. How we view the people on the waiting list and the potential client trying to circumvent the list, whether as intimates or strangers, will influence the ethical action we take.

Toulmin (1981) distinguishes between ethics toward family members and ethics toward strangers. We relate differently to families, intimates, and neighbors than to complete strangers. In transient encounters our moral obligations are limited to avoid acting in an offensive manner. For example, when waiting to see a movie, one does not go to the head of the line, but waits one's turn. "So, in the ethics of strangers, respect for rules is all, and the opportunities for discretion are few. In the ethics of intimacy, discretion is all, and the relevance of strict rules is minimal" (p. 34).

It is necessary to classify the intimates and the strangers in this scenario. An influential person has called the federation professional about a certain individual in order to circumvent the waiting list. The potential client is an intimate to the caller, but a stranger to the professional, as are all the people on the waiting list. The caller, as a colleague or friend, is in the category of intimate to the professional.

Who is the professional's client? Is the client the caller or the person who desires admission to the nursing home? To the professional, the person is a stranger, the caller an intimate. Toward strangers, "respect for rules is all," and the rule is to abide by the waiting list. Toward intimates, "discretion is all," and the rules may be bent. What is the ethical thing to do?

Were we to agree that the professional's client is the caller, and apply the ethics of intimacy and thereby legitimate the circumvention, it could be countered that the client is the group seeking entry into the nursing home and only the home has jurisdiction over its admissions policy. The home is currently filled to capacity and there is a waiting list. As clients-to-be, all the people on the waiting list may be categorized as strangers who will have to abide by the institution's rules and policies. The caller and the professional are distant players on this scene who may not ethically influence decisions on admission. Since there is a waiting list of "strangers," respect for rules is paramount.

Respect for rules should ideally govern federation-agency relationships. In breaking the rules, federation creates an expectation that agencies kowtow to its demands, thus fostering a negative impact on the relationship.

ETHICAL THEORY

With the values of justice and preferred conceptions of the client providing one conceptual framework, ethical theory can provide another conceptual framework for this ethical dilemma. Since an ethical dilemma is based on conflicting values, the professional inevitably experiences ambivalence as to the proper action in the situation. The ambivalence may be exacerbated by several variables: the security of the professional's job in the agency, the strength of the power being exerted, the consequences of nonacquiescence, and the depth of the professional's relationship with the caller. These variables are based on different assumptions.

A professional who feels insecure in the job will more likely succumb to the pressure of circumventing the waiting list than one who feels secure in the job. Yet, even the professional with longevity and a sense of security may not be able to resist the repeated demands of a powerful lay person. The consequences of refusal may be the loss of one's job, reduction or withdrawal of the gift to the campaign, and resigning from the agency's board. The strength of the lay person's power is a function of his or her status in the community; the higher the status, the greater the power, and the more wrenching the refusal. Refusal is also a function of the relationship between the lay person and the professional; the deeper the relationship, the greater the sense of obligation to acquiesce. Ultimately, the central question is, what is the right/ good thing to do?

A grasp of these variables is essential in order to apply ethical theory to this dilemma. The conflict between the right and the good can be located in the conflict between the deontological and utilitarian approaches to ethics. Table 6 illustrates the application of these ethical theories to the case illustration.

Table 6: Application of Ethical Theory to Circumventing the Waiting List

Ethical Theory	Circumvent	Do Not Circumvent
Deontological	Duty of non-maleficence; duty of gratitude to donor	Duty of fidelity to people on waiting list; principle of "first come, first served"
Utilitarian	Retain lay leader's involvement in agency; preserve agency's financial viability; prevent loss of professional's job	Person waiting may die—greater harm principle; public protest

Deontologists posit the inherent rightness of an action for reasons other than its consequences, such as intuition and common sense. They contend that there are several basic moral principles or prima facie duties, such as fidelity, nonmaleficence, beneficence, and justice, which justify moral action (Beauchamp and Childress 1994). These duties are also in the category of ethical principles that guide action. It would appear that circumventing the waiting list is simply wrong because the others were there first and the duty of fidelity prevails. Yet, the principle of "first come, first served" may not be the only one applicable in this situation. The degree of need, especially when there is a threat to life, may supersede that principle. It is conceivable that the person being pushed to the front of the waiting list is more needy than the others. Deontologists might incline in that direction due to the prima facie duty of nonmaleficence (preventing harm), which, to Ross, supersedes the duty of fidelity. Intuition in one direction can be reversed toward the opposite direction by additional information.

Utilitarians maintain that the moral rightness of an action is determined by its consequences. The consequences of an act, however, are unpredictable and subject to disagreement. At issue in these cases are the possible consequences of refusal. The individual might die. The professional may lose his or her job. The caller may reduce or eliminate the gift, may sever the friendship, may resign from the federation. If the caller is a major donor, the loss may be keenly felt. Since these negative consequences may be harmful to more people than the refusal to place one person at the head of the list, utilitarian thinking would opt for giving in to the caller's demand. The act of acquiescence can be viewed as good because it is based on the prevention of greater harm.

Consideration needs to be given to the possible negative effects of acquiescence. It is conceivable that the person superseded on the waiting list is in more dire need than the caller's relative, and the delay in institutionalization may hasten death. Moreover, though such decisions are usually made with discretion and in private, the action may become known in the community and generate public protest. Thus, to avoid these negative consequences, it is necessary to resist the pressure. By insisting on an ethical standard of fairness, the professional adds to the credibility and authenticity of the agency and the profession.

The deontological-utilitarian framework may also be applied to the value conflict of justice versus fiscal adequacy. Deontologists could maintain that the waiting list should be inviolate because the agency has established a relationship of trust with the people awaiting entry. The prima facie duties of justice and fidelity to the people on the waiting list may override the intrusion of a new person with whom there is no prior relationship (Pritchard 1912).

On the other hand, the prima facie duty of gratitude could be operating here. Federation executives often convey to large contributors and board members that they can expect preferential treatment for members of their families, whether in the use of services or gaining employment. There is an implicit promise that they will be served ahead of others. In an informal survey conducted at one federation, the majority of board members indicated that they expected such "perks." The professional feels a sense of duty to fulfill these unwritten promises.

Utilitarians could maintain that the fiscal viability of the agency supports the duty of gratitude and supersedes the duties of justice and fidelity. If the consequence of refusal is the withdrawal of financial support, and thus a possible threat to fiscal solvency, then refusal is unethical as it causes greater harm.

The ambivalence of the federation professionals in the two cases about circumventing the waiting list may be attributed to numerous variables and different philosophical approaches. Deontological and utilitarian theories do not lead to particular conflict resolutions, but they can be utilized, in conjunction with ethical principles, to support the pros and cons of each side. They facilitate the exploration of options and locate them in a conceptual base. Since, by definition, more than one option exists in ethically ambiguous situations, it is difficult to maintain a consistent stance in all instances. Ideally, a professional's ethical instincts should deem the waiting list inviolate, but it may be difficult to withstand the pressure of influential lay people.

CONCLUSION

Circumventing the waiting list as an ethical dilemma was designed to serve as a model for analyzing conflicting values and theories. Analysis focused on overriding or acquiescing to the caller's request. If the request is denied based on ethical considerations, another approach may be taken. The federation executive and the caller can meet with the prospective entrant to explore alternative actions. This gesture recognizes the power and affluence of the caller, and the importance of the request for service. It also maintains the integrity of the home for the aged by affirming its ethical responsibility to the waiting list. Efforts should be made to create other opportunities for the caller to continue his/her leadership role in the federation.

In some Jewish communities, two waiting lists are formed. Most of the admissions come from the "regular" waiting list. The remainder are reserved for lay leaders who have helped to create the facility—major donors to the home, trustees, key professionals, and government personnel. Communities need to be innovative in accommodating the needs of the people on the waiting list and the relatives of community leaders.

The hallmark of a professional is action that proceeds from a rational process of deliberation. To analyze and resolve ethical dilemmas requires concerted thinking, a readiness to weigh the many variables and values in the conflict, and a tolerance for ambiguity.

Chapter 9

Fund-raising

Fund-raising activities, particularly in federations, are permeated with ethical dilemmas. Federations began as central fund-raising organizations that attempted to bring together the fund-raising campaigns of different organizations in the Jewish community. The centrality of this function became solidified when the United Jewish Appeal merged its campaign with those of the local federations.

Of the many ethical issues that emerge in the course of raising funds, four have been selected for analysis. The first offers a glimpse into the agony of a Jewishly committed fund-raiser. The middle two deal with wealthy individuals whose power contravenes agency policy. The last presents ethical situations with regard to bequests and endowments.

FUND-RAISING FOR ISRAEL

I have an ethical dilemma as a fund raiser/social worker during the Israel crisis. Crisis is good for fund-raising because historically we always make more money in times of crisis; part of me even hopes for one.

As a Jew, a child of Holocaust survivors, and a social worker, I feel troubled and guilty over my hoping for a crisis in Israel. Every time a Scud missile is shot at Israel, it's another $10,000 in the bank. It is unfortunate that the people to whom we reach out need something like that to motivate them to get closer to Israel and to their Jewish roots. I find myself in a serious ethical conflict regarding my wanting to raise as much money as I can but in order to do so, I hope for a dangerous situation in Israel.

We have had the Israel Emergency Fund, Operation Moses for the Ethiopian Jews, Passage to Freedom for the resettlement of Soviet Jews here, and Operation Exodus. Every time we have one of those second-line campaigns, they more than prove to be very successful. The money just keeps on flowing in.

The conflict is between the value of wanting to help people here, in Israel, and in thirty-four countries versus raising money at all costs and whatever it takes.

Discussion

Since the conflict is not interpersonal but internal, the professional does not have an ethical dilemma. As we pointed out earlier, ethical dilemmas emanate only from interpersonal relationships. There is no conflict here with the people of Israel, nor with the donors to the campaigns. The conflict is between two personal values: wanting to help Jews wherever they live, and hoping for a life-threatening crisis so that more money could be raised.

It is an agonizing dilemma because several identities of this professional are in conflict. As a child of Holocaust survivors, he is more sensitive than the average Jew to attempts to annihilate Jews. He also views Israel as a place of refuge for the survivors of the Holocaust and for persecuted Jews from Ethiopia, the Soviet Union, and other countries. His fund-raising activities are motivated by his desire to ensure the survival of Israel and of Jews wherever they live.

The professional is also a community social worker in an organization dedicated to the survival and enhancement of Jewish life here and abroad. His objective is to raise as much money as he can in order to achieve these purposes. A crisis situation increases the success of the campaign. He is torn when he hopes for a crisis to his people in order to obtain greater support for them. He continues to live with the agony of the dilemma.

The professional's dilemma is an outgrowth of the unfortunate way campaigns have been structured—on the back of Israel. An Israeli educator once remarked sarcastically that UJA needs wars in Israel in order for its campaigns to succeed. Campaigns need to find broader themes and a common base that may include, but not be limited to, Israel. Operation Exodus is a good example. It showed that extraordinary amounts of money can be raised without a physical threat to Israel. The combination of potential threat in the former Soviet Union along with the Zionist dream of the ingathering of the exiles resulted in an outpouring of funds heretofore not seen during peacetime.The dilemma has not been resolved.

"MONEY TALKS"

There is a major contributor who has given us millions of dollars and solicited millions more, whose spouse has become the associate director of an agency that we fund. While we are cutting back our agency allocations, this contributor wants his wife's agency to get a 100 percent increase in the grant.

It is an ethical problem from the point of view of equity. It is unfair for an agency to receive a 100 percent increase when other agencies are being decreased. On the other hand, this person has made it very clear that he will walk away from federation if we refuse. We stand to lose millions of dollars. The ethical dilemma is made slightly less unpalatable by the fact that his wife's agency provides good services. If it did not, it would be a devastating ethical dilemma because it would be more difficult to justify the increase.

To resolve this, I talked to three supervisors. One of them said we are being held up, this is a robbery, and I am not sure there is anything we can do about it. The other supervisor characterized it as the old question of where does the 600-pound gorilla sit—wherever it wants. The third person said, "Sometimes you just have to lie back and enjoy it." The fund-raising department urged us to do whatever this person wants, as we cannot risk the impact on the campaign.

Knowing the wife's agency's program is decent enables me to rationalize that we are not losing funds that help people in Israel, but I am still troubled by it. The total grant, including the 100 percent increase, is under $150,000, so that the allocation increase is about $75,000. I would probably make the same decision.

Discussion

This case concerns a donor asking for an increase for his wife's agency, but such dilemmas take other forms too. Examples include lay leaders who want their relatives to circumvent the waiting list in a nursing home, or demand that the agency purchase supplies from their businesses, or that the agency hire their relatives for jobs. This case is a paradigm of the lay person's exercise of power for personal and family gain.

The resolution applied utilitarian reasoning. Staff was persuaded that the gentleman would carry out his threat to leave federation if his request were denied. Federation stood to lose tens of millions of dollars by not acceding to his request. The greater good was served by granting the increase, although it violated federation policy of allocation reductions. The contributions made by this donor, as well as those solicited by him, outweighed the cost of the inequitable decision, and contributed to the greater good. The prima facie duty of gratitude took precedence over the prima facie duty of justice.

Another approach is to assist the agency to secure resources from other sources. This may not satisfy the donor, but if his major concern is to increase the budgetary allotment to his wife's agency, he may be persuaded to pursue other available resources and not demand that federation increase its allocation.

DONOR PREFERENCE VS. AGENCY POLICY

A major donor has requested that 100 percent of his gift to Operation Exodus be sent directly to Israel to benefit Jews from the former Soviet Union. None of it is to be used to resettle them in the local community. Our federation policy states that 75 percent of contributions to Operation Exodus are sent to Israel and 25 percent remain for local resettlement. If we insist on maintaining agency policy, he will withhold his gift. What is the right thing to do?

Discussion

In this ethical dilemma, there is a conflict between two values. One value is to accept the gift to benefit Jews in Israel and retain this contributor for the federation campaign. Another value is to affirm agency policy that supports resettlement efforts in the local community.

Ethical theory and principles could be used to justify both values. The ultimate decision depends on balancing the relative weights of one principle over the other (Beauchamp and Childress 1994). Deontological theory supports the ethics of an action based on common sense and on the prior relationship with the individual. A long-standing relationship has developed between federation and this donor, who has been active on committees and has contributed to many campaigns. The prima facie duty of gratitude and the principle of respect for autonomy could justify agreement with the donor's stipulation. This is his will, and while it violates agency policy, his intentions are noble.

Utilitarian theory could also justify the decision to accept the condition of the gift. Since all of it goes to Israel, it conduces to the greater good; if the condition is declined, the gift is too, leading to harm. The principles here are respect for autonomy and avoidance of nonmaleficence.

Contrary considerations could sway the executive to reject the gift. From a deontological perspective, federation's allegiance to Jews from the former Soviet Union in the local community takes priority over their compatriots in Israel. The local relationship preceded the overseas one. This can also be supported by the talmudic dictum that giving to the poor of one's city precedes giving to the poor of another city. If the condition of the gift is accepted, funds from other donors have to be shifted from the standard percentage distribution to conform to the policy. This would not be fair to the other contributors, who think that most of it goes to Israel.

From a utilitarian perspective, negative consequences could ensue were the gift to be accepted as stipulated. A precedent would be established that might be emulated by other contributors. This would make the policy erratic, and local immigrants would be deprived of services. Federation would be constantly redistributing funds in order to accommodate the 75–25 percentage distribution which it had established. The decision to accept the gift under these conditions would, therefore, be unethical.

Decision

Federation decided to accept the donor's gift along with the condition. It reasoned that accepting the gift helped more people, and that it was more important to retain the loyalty of the donor than to alienate him. Considerations with regard to possible negative consequences were less weighty than the benefits to be accrued. The decision was justified by the principle of respect for autonomy and the prima facie duty of gratitude, and supported by deontological and utilitarian theories.

Many agencies would similarly agree to the donor's stipulation, but would adjust the total sums. This is akin to double-entry bookkeeping. In essence, the donor's preference is not really honored.

BEQUESTS AND ENDOWMENTS

The director of a federation's department of bequests and endowments offered a number of interrelated ethical situations. Some of the dilemmas could be resolved either way, while others posed right and wrong options.

Case I

We provide direct services for a donor's financial, estate, and tax needs. As a consequence, a great many older individuals rely on me as their professional advisor. They have begun to look life in the eye and want to do something to preserve their immortality. They have connected directly or loosely to this organization or to the Jewish people. Oftentimes they are alone, have a great deal of accumulated wealth, and have never given to charity before.

As we develop a plan which I am convinced is good for them economically, taxwise, and philanthropically, I notice that I am becoming their professional advisor. I encourage them to have an attorney or an accountant review the ideas and recommend their implementation. If they do not have one, I offer them a list of lawyers whom they could call. Oftentimes these donors say they do not have a lawyer nor an accountant and they want me to serve in those capacities. After working with these people over many months, I am in the position of becoming their surrogate advisor, their surrogate son. It is an awfully difficult ethical situation.

When some realize that they have to get another advisor, it is very confusing for them. It implies that they cannot trust me completely. They are not sophisticated enough to know that there is an ethical problem here.

Do I tell them that I will not work for them further because I represent federation and cannot represent them? Having given them the opportunity to have a lawyer and an accountant and they turned it down, do I continue to work with them conscientiously because there is a benefit to both parties in the transaction? Or do I simply avoid the issue altogether by doing what I think is right for them and for the organization without even mentioning the ethical considerations?

There have been times when I made a judgment to complete the transaction because not to do it would be more wrong. I wrestled with the idea, checked into my own soul, and concluded that it was right. Ethically, one might conclude that it was a violation of the rules, not because the result was wrong. There are occasions when I have to look at it in terms of the total good.

This is a conflict because one cannot represent both sides to a transaction, even if the transaction is not adversarial. Any product that is of benefit to them will have a concurrent benefit to federation. I believe that I have been completely fair, equitable, and objective. However, there is a perception that I am representing two parties with different interests, though I am convinced that I am looking out particularly for the donor. Therefore, I am caught in this dilemma.

Discussion

The professional is clear about his role with donors. He represents the federation and is not their personal advisor/lawyer/accountant. It is in federation's interests to obtain the largest bequest or endowment possible to maintain its fiscal viability and serve the Jewish community.

The donor is the agency's client whose vulnerability evokes the professional's ethical sensitivities (Lewis 1986; Levy 1982). Vulnerability is manifested in the client's advanced age, a lack of knowledge of planned giving, and a lack of connection with the organized Jewish community. The client's best interests are at stake and require special sensitivity by the professional.

The professional's dilemma is that he cannot represent federation and the client at the same time. The proposed resolution is simple. The donor should hire a lawyer or accountant to represent him, thereby freeing the professional to represent the federation alone, and avoid the conflict of interests. The dilemma surfaces when the donor refuses to do so and, instead, asks the professional to represent him.

Sometimes the professional will make the transaction for the donor without the benefit of a financial advisor. Guided by utilitarian motives, he believes that this action promotes the donor's long-term interests. Act-utilitarianism supports the violation of rules when the act will conduce to the greater good (Beauchamp and Childress 1994).

The professional opts to try to distinguish between the donor's interests and the agency's interests. He will trust his judgment and his ethical sensitivities, and will be guided by the principle of nonmaleficence in dealing with vulnerable clients.

There are a number of variables that help the professional to decide when to act on behalf of clients. If there are family members who might attack the will or the transactions, he will not take the initiative, as it could cause many problems for the federation. If it is clear that no accusations of undue influence on donors will be forthcoming, because they are alone or their families agree that the decisions are in the donor's best interests, the professional will take the initiative.

The professional has established a consultation system with lawyers to review the dilemmas and confirm the ethics of his actions. "It would be ethically questionable for me to take the donor through the transaction, absent some oversight by an independent advisor."

Case II
I will oftentimes turn down a gift if I think it is ethically ques-

tionable or not in the best interests of the donor, even though it may be wonderful for federation.

A donor wants me to invest his money in a trust which would provide a regular income for him. I believe that this is not in his best interests, as he may want to take a trip or buy a home and his capital would be tied up in the trust. In the long run, our relationship will be better served by telling him that it is not good for him, because he will invest it anyway in another form. It is always in the organization's best interest, but it may not always be in the donor's best interest.

Discussion

The ethical sensitivity of the professional is demonstrated again in this case. It is always in the interests of the federation to receive investments, but it may not always be in the interests of donors. They tend to be unsophisticated in financial planning, and vulnerable to deception.

The professional used his knowledge of consequences to help the client anticipate the outcomes of his decision. Practically, the federation lost the investment, but ethically it was the right thing to do. In this case, the professional's ethical responsibility prevailed.

Case III

There are people who want to make a gift but cannot because they are clearly incompetent. I deem it wrong to take the gift. However, if we believe they understand, are lucid, and it is in their economic best interest, and by not doing it, it would be very costly from a tax point of view, then it may be okay to accept the gift. This is a large gray area where each donor needs to be individualized.

Discussion

This case evokes complex issues of client competence and informed consent. In the bioethical literature, these issues are discussed under the ethical principle of respect for autonomy (Beauchamp and Childress 1994). The principle that guides the professional is his respect for the autonomy of the donor who is making major financial decisions. The professional wants to be

certain that the donor understands the ramifications of these decisions. If he deems the donor to be incompetent, he will not proceed with a plan. If he deems the donor to be competent, he will
provide information regarding the plan, and want to be assured
that it is understood before consent is given.

Case IV

A 65-year-old man, ill with terminal cancer, wanted to create
a charitable trust. The transaction was approved by our lawyer and his lawyer. While in the hospital, he decided to add
his daughter, whom he had wanted to disinherit, as a secondary beneficiary.

We really anguished about this. On the one hand, it was a
completed, irrevocable trust with $500,000–$600,000 for federation. By his adding the daughter as a beneficiary, the
money would be deferred for perhaps fifty years.

Do I allow that trust to be amended because he wants it or
do I not? I could not decide. Federation said not to change it.
My humanistic half said I should. My committee chairman
and I decided that since we are serving this donor and this
was his request, and his doctors said he is competent, we did
it. I gave up the present value of half a million dollars.

Discussion

The professional's ethical dilemma is based on a conflict of values.
The value of self-determination affirms the client's ethical right to
change the designation of his beneficiaries, though legally he may
not, for he had created an irrevocable trust. Federation values fiscal stability, which would deny the request to change the trust.
Since the deal was mutually agreed upon by lawyers for both parties, it should not be changed because it is a "done deal."

Ethically, there is a conflict of rules, principles, and justifications
by ethical theories. From the client's perspective, the professional
is guided by the rule to abide by the client's wishes because he ini-
tiated the transaction. This is justified by the principle of respect
for client autonomy. The principle, in turn, can be supported by
deontological theory, which posits the professional's prima facie
duty of fidelity to the client based on their relationship. Deontologically, it is common sense that a person should be able to

change his mind regarding a contract before it becomes effective.

From the agency's perspective, the rule that guides the professional-client relationship is that a signed document must be honored. This can be justified by the principle of fidelity to federation, based on the client's having given his word and entered into a mutual agreement. The principle can be supported by deontological theory. It is commonsensical that a signed agreement is final.

Utilitarian theory could also be applied via the principle of utility—the promotion of the greater good for the greatest number. If federation could have the money now instead of waiting for fifty years, it would redound to the immediate benefit of the local and international Jewish community. This good is greater than the good produced for the daughter.

The dilemma was resolved in favor of the donor and supported by deontological thinking. The professional and the chairman emphasized the prior relationship with the donor, and the need to respect his autonomy. They were not driven by greed. The decision was very costly to federation, but it was deemed to be the ethical thing to do. The moral traces that remained in the decision not taken were very costly financially and emotionally.

CONCLUSION

In raising funds for Israel during a time of crisis, professionals may find themselves in a wrenching conflict. If one's heart is in the task, one cannot help but agonize over the terrible dilemma that ensues when the amount of money raised is proportional to the intensity of the crisis. It is a commonplace that success in fund-raising occurs "on the back of Israel," a common complaint of Israelis. But such is the nature of fund-raising that Jews do not respond to solicitations unless a crisis exists. Professionals will continue to live with this agonizing conflict.

The impact of wealthy donors on agency policy is reflected in the second and third cases. Professionals are faced with serious ethical concerns over circumventing federation policy to accommodate donors' requests. The decision to do so appears to be rationalized in order to obtain the gift, but it was also supported by ethical theory and justified by ethical principles.

In the area of bequests and endowments, intense relationships develop between professionals and donors that differ markedly from ordinary fund-raising relationships, which, with some exceptions, tend to be superficial. Fund-raisers do not become involved in family dynamics, estate planning, or financial conditions of donors. Because relationships between professionals and donors become intense in the process of making bequests or wills, professionals feel a deeper commitment to meet the needs of donors and incline toward their interests in doubtful situations. The ethical bulb illuminates the appropriate response.

Chapter 10

Distributing Funds to Agencies

Federation's role in distributing funds to its constituent agencies is fraught with ethical dilemmas. This chapter is not primarily concerned with the ethical dilemmas attendant to the allocation of scarce resources, but with choice—the hard choices that need to be made whenever funds are to be distributed to a variety of agencies with different ideologies, and to Israel.

Three dilemmas are cited. The first presents ethical considerations related to maintaining agencies in changing communities. The second questions a federation's right to allocate money directly to Israel and bypass the Jewish Agency. The third discusses the priority of funding services for Jews or leveraging public funds in order to serve the general community too.

CONSOLIDATING AGENCIES IN A CHANGING COMMUNITY

> We support a network of affiliated agencies that have votes on our assembly and are key to the governing structure of the federation. We are committed to fund them and to ensure their success. We also have a commitment to our contributors to ensure Jewish continuity, and provide services to client populations designated by our donors.
>
> The dilemma is whether finite resources are best spread over all our agencies or whether they can be more efficiently administered in a smaller group of agencies.
>
> There are really two competing questions. How many agencies are needed to provide significant services? What is

the extent of our responsibility to our affiliated organizations?

Two agencies whose programs, government auspices, and
grant-making agency (federation) are the same, are providing similar services in adjacent communities. Some real econ-
omies could be developed if these two agencies merged or
their services were rationalized. Federation can exercise
moral and fiscal persuasion in bringing together agencies
that are providing similar services.

Can we provide the services with half the number of agencies? Are we breaching the compact made with our affiliated
agencies by trying to get some of them to go out of existence
so that the entire community can be strengthened? That is
more of an ethical or moral dilemma. It is more acute now
because we are in the process of recommending to the board
a significantly reduced level of funding for next year.

True decision-making is not made by professionals here,
but by the lay leadership. What I and my staff try to do is to
sharpen the issues, to make sure the decision-making process
is well informed, that the agencies are given the opportunity
to present their case fairly, that their numbers and their nar-
ratives and their budget proposals are presented properly to
those in positions of authority to make decisions on funding.

Budget analysis is very much like any other analysis in that
it is not completely value-free. When trying to make a point,
one makes it from a perspective. The key is balance, fairness,
or justification. Decisions are made by the leadership, and
the range of concerns about issues and priorities and mission
are not ethical dilemmas for me personally. I do not have to
worry whether the Jewish education agencies get funded less
than the family services agencies. My interest is in making
sure that there is a level playing field, that the concerns of the
agencies and their presentations are heard and threaded
equally and fairly.

If I make the recommendation to the committee on how I
think grants should be administered, how funds should be
released and reconciled, whether we should pay overhead,
whether we should provide reimbursement after the fact,
advances before the fact, what our reserves look like, and

how we should use our resources to fund next year's grants—those are financial and management issues. They are not issues of program, policy, and ethics.

Discussion

Sometimes ethical dilemmas are resolved not by individuals but by circumstances. In this case, the circumstances are forcing difficult decisions to be made. There is a shortfall in funds, cuts in agency allocations are being recommended across the board, and the possibility of eliminating agencies is real. Ethical guidelines may be found in Jewish tradition and ethical theory to inform decisions in these cases.

The Bible says that one is supposed to give to the poor "sufficient for his need" (Deuteronomy 15:8). In discussing the meaning of "sufficient," the Talmud enunciates the principle that "you are commanded to maintain him, but you are not commanded to make him rich" (Talmud Ketubot 67b). "Maintaining" would seem to require the federation to continue to support these agencies, even though less will be allocated than last year. "Making rich" could refer to federation's combining agencies at the expense of those being closed. Therefore, since the obligation is to maintain and not make rich, federation should continue the current agency structure.

The reverse may be more ethical. Maintaining requires that the level of services to which the community has been accustomed be continued in the most effective and efficient manner. If this requires consolidation, so be it. Alternatively, keeping agencies in business when they are no longer viable may fall into the category of making them rich—expending more money than is necessary. Consequently, no clear direction can be derived from the talmudic principle concerning the ethical action to be taken.

The dilemma could also be analyzed by resorting to ethical principles and prima facie duties. A principle is a guide to action, and a duty is an imperative to action. The ethical literature generally utilizes principles, whereas Ross (1930) uses prima facie duties which are more focused in given situations. Federation has longstanding relationships with each of the agencies in the community. Loyalty has been built up over many years of working together; therefore, the duty of fidelity insists that these relationships continue through adequate levels of funding. A contrary principle and prima facie duty is justice. Federation is duty-bound to ask whether it is fair to maintain agencies that are no longer viable when there is a shortage of funds. The fairness principle (Beauchamp and Childress 1994) addresses the just distribution of scarce resources.

In his analysis of conflicting prima facie duties, Ross (1930) suggests that the claim of each duty needs to be weighed and a decision will follow. He offers no objective criteria for weighing and decision-making. In this case, there is a conflict between fidelity to the existing agencies and the just distribution of limited funds. Each claims that federation uphold its prima facie duty. How shall federation be guided in the resolution of the dilemma? One approach is to examine the policies that will accompany the restructuring.

The new policy advocates an improvement in services through a change in structure. The merging of agencies assures the uninterrupted continuity of services to the community. It results in more, not less, service being delivered. Mergers, combinations, and consolidations tend to result in eliminating administrative overhead functions. There is one executive director, instead of two. A single accounting, public relations, facilities management, and supervisory structure replaces the two that were previously in place. The savings are then able to be reinvested in client services. There is, then, an imperative to move in the direction of consolidation .

This policy resolves the dilemma. The prima facie duty of justice, the fairness principle, is joined by the principle and duty of beneficence to justify consolidation. This conclusion is also consistent with utilitarian theory, which seeks to promote the greatest good for the greatest number. The dilemma seems to be more clearly resolved through the application of ethical principles and theory than the talmudic principle.

DISTRIBUTING FUNDS IN ISRAEL

Federations have a long-standing policy that funds raised for Israel are turned over to the Jewish Agency for distribution in Israel. Allocation decisions are left up to the Jewish Agency's discretion, for it presumably knows the country's needs better than others and is working in Israel's best interests. However, a federation has begun to question this common belief.

> In my division, we want to have greater input in the distribution of the funds to projects that we deem to be important. We believe that sometimes our judgment is better than that of the Jewish Agency. This brings us into conflict with the prevailing value regarding the greater expertise of the Jewish Agency staff. By this action, we are accused of severing ourselves from the mainstream of United Jewish Appeal agencies, which is not our aim.
>
> For example, we were asked by the mayor of a town in Israel to fund a certain project. We thought that the project was worthwhile, and supporting that mayor would create new leadership for Israel's future. The leaders of the Jewish Agency accused us of helping a well-established town, instead of the very needy.
>
> Our position is that we are equals in this enterprise. Each of us has something to contribute to make Israel strong. The Jewish Agency may know the conditions in Israel far better than we, but we can have a more objective understanding of Jewish continuity. The Israeli system chokes the individual. In little ways we are trying to transform Israeli society by influencing one mayor in one town. We are going to make a difference.
>
> The ethical dilemma is whether we are creating a schism in the unity of the Jewish people by bucking the established system.

Discussion

Federation's desire to assert independence appears to clash with the Jewish Agency's desire to hold onto its power. Federation's value is in asserting greater control over the distribution of funds; the Jewish Agency's value is in maintaining control over the traditional partnership between United States Jews and Israel.

The essence of the conflict is: whose money is it, the Jewish Agency's or the federation's? Federation has raised it from individuals who have donated it to Israel, so that Israel has a claim on it. In classic Jewish tradition, the money that an individual gives to *tzedakah* has actually been designated to the recipient; the donor serves as an intermediary between God and the recipient (Talmud Ketubot 67b). The Jewish Agency claims that it is the intermediary through which the funds will be channeled to the people of Israel. Federation contends that the fund-raising organization is the intermediary between the donors and the people of Israel, and it should have jurisdiction over the distribution.

The conflict of values leads to a conflict between the ethical principle of respect for autonomy and paternalism, an exaggerated form of the principle of beneficence. Federation would like the Jewish Agency to respect its autonomy in the distribution of funds. Resentment is directed toward the Jewish Agency's paternalistic attitude in making the allocation decisions by itself.

The conflict may also be located within utilitarian theory. Federation believes that it contributes to the greater good by controlling the distribution of funds. In the words of the professional, "I feel I know the system, the culture, the issues of Israeli society, and I know what my community needs and wants as well." The desire for the power of the purse aims to enhance daily life in Israel.

The Jewish Agency claims that it contributes to the greater good through the current system. As an organization indigenous to Israeli society, the Jewish Agency was established to resettle immigrants and build the infrastructure of the country. Promoting the greater good of the Israeli people is its raison d'etre. Morally, it claims that it owns the funds because they were raised "on the backs of Israel."

In the Talmud, when one person claims that another owes him money, the dispute is resolved with the principle *hamotzi me'chavero alav ha'rayah*—"the one trying to extract the money must bring proof that it is his." In applying this principle, it is clear that federation possesses the funds because it collected them. The Jewish Agency, in its efforts to extract the funds, needs to demonstrate that its distribution plan is better.

There is a strong belief, confirmed by experience, that lay involvement in the allocations process leads to greater involvement in giving and soliciting. The consequence would be more funds for the Jewish Agency and for direct allocations by federation.

The professional deems it ethical for federation to circumvent the Jewish Agency and select its own projects for funding in Israel. The value of self-determination is supported by the ethical principles of autonomy and utility—the promotion of the greater good for Israelis and lay leaders.

LEVERAGING GOVERNMENT FUNDS TO SERVE THE BROADER COMMUNITY

The following ethical dilemma pervades federation work, and challenges the values and skills of the professionals involved.

The Jewish community has a limited amount of money available for distribution to agencies. The ethical dilemma for me is: should we give the money raised from the Jewish community to those agencies that serve only Jews, i.e., a Jewish dollar for a Jewish service, or should we give it to agencies in order to leverage money from government sources, i.e., a Jewish dollar that brings down non-Jewish money, which then allows the agency to serve the general population as well as the Jewish community? Some would say that more Jews are served that way than if we just directed the money only for Jewish services and Jewish people. What is the right way to allocate money raised from the Jewish community?

One variable is the type of agency being funded. Jewish education and camping are strengthening Jewish life, with very limited resources from non-Jewish funds. They value Jews perpetuating their own survival. We need to have some influence outside the community to protect us from external dangers. When it serves all people, is a Jewish agency different from a Catholic or Protestant agency? Jews value survival, protection, the need to influence and communicate with the rest of the world, and not to be insulated. In our tradition, we attribute significant value to helping others.

A second variable is the accuracy of the reports submitted by the agencies on the use of the money and the numbers of Jews served through leveraging. We want to be certain that the money is not serving more non-Jews than Jews.

There are basically two types of grants: basic and

restricted. Basic grants match government money and central administrative costs. Restrictive grants, from foundations and endowments, are meant to serve only Jews, such as the frail Jewish elderly. Money given through the basic grant can be used in any way. An agency can use it for leveraging, for central administrative costs, and for direct services to Jews.

A third variable is the agency's presentation before the distribution committee, whether its commitment is to the Jewish community or to the agency. For federation, the first issue is not the survival of the agency but the survival of the Jewish community and how the agency serves that purpose. An agency should not say it is using this money to strengthen the Jewish community if it cannot prove the case.

My struggle is how to achieve a balance in guiding my committee to distribute its money. It must serve Jews both directly, through cash maintenance, counseling, and all of the social service programs, and at the same time be aware that we must be serving the general community.

Discussion

What appears to be an ethical dilemma is based on a seeming conflict of values. Should grants be given only to serve Jews, or should they also be given to leverage funds from government sources to serve both Jews and non-Jews? Federation values serving Jews and serving the general community that includes Jews. Both values are perceived to perpetuate Jewish survival. There is, therefore, no ethical dilemma, because both values contribute to Jewish survival and are implemented in the allocations process.

> In communicating with agencies, we insist that the value of serving the Jewish community and the value of trying to increase funding by leveraging be honored. We are not inclined towards one value as opposed to the other.

The Mission Statement of one federation does not mention Jews in its aim of helping "individuals and families in need—the old and young, the unemployed, the homeless, the sick and the poor—and to resettle those who are persecuted or oppressed" (UJA 1993, p. 5).

Yet, the balance is not even, for serving Jews is a higher priority. It is listed as the first item in the Mission Statement of the same federation: "To ensure the continuity of the Jewish people, to enhance the quality of Jewish life" (UJA 1993, p. 5). Four funding criteria designed to inform allocations decisions are directed to Jewish services, while two extend beyond Jewish services (ibid., pp. 7–8).

The respondent corroborated this priority: "The political considerations of working with the general community are extremely important, but not of a higher value than how many Jews are being served." The purpose of leveraging is ultimately designed to help the Jewish community. "It is one way to help this community survive. It is a very powerful tool." The Jewish community recognizes an obligation to the general community, and that its own sustenance is based, in part, on general community conditions.

The continuity of a strong Jewish community requires both the internal educational components to assure a desire for communal maintenance, along with the external conditions of stability, a strong economy, and comfort. These factors contribute to the resolution of the value conflict: the priority is to serve Jews, but there is an obligation to serve the general community too. This position is consistent with Judaism's insistence that the non-Jewish poor be served because of *darkei shalom*—maintaining peace in the community.

Along with the moral obligation and the need for communal stability, fiscal solvency drives the resolution of the value conflict. Agencies that have been relying on public funds to meet their budget commitments are receiving less because of cutbacks in public funding, even as federations have reduced their allocations. This has imposed severe hardships for budgets and services. Even if federations wanted to serve only Jews, funds from the Jewish community are inadequate. Leveraging seems to be the only hope for agencies to survive, short of considerable downsizing, which they are reluctant to do.

CONCLUSION

Three ethical dilemmas have highlighted fundamental value conflicts in federation's social planning for the local Jewish community, the general community, and Israel. The ongoing conflicts continue to confront lay and professional leaders in various forms. Analysis of these dilemmas points to the need to discern underlying values and ethical principles in order to determine priorities in the distribution of scarce funds when the demographic complexion of a community changes, when autonomy in allocating funds to Israeli institutions is asserted, and when Jewish funds are leveraged in order to bring in public funds to support local services.

Chapter 11

Talmudic and Ethical Approaches to Resettlement of Jews from the Former Soviet Union

The continuing exodus of Jews from the former Soviet Union to the United States has strained communal budgets and staff deployment, and necessitated the establishment of special Project Exodus fund-raising campaigns, social planning and services among federations, agencies, and the Council of Jewish Federations. A plan, "Equitable Collective Responsibility," was developed whereby every Jewish community has agreed to resettle Russian refugees or contribute funds to those communities that do resettle them. Federations agreed to this plan in proportion to the size of their Jewish population and annual campaign. As a result of lower campaign collections, contributions have decreased. The United States government's per capita contribution has been the same for the last few years, and this, too, might cease if the refugee status of these Jews is rescinded. There is a growing perception that Jews from the former Soviet Union are not in as life-threatening situations as other refugees, such as Bosnians.

These Jews would then be considered immigrants, and not eligible for public assistance benefits. Their support would totally devolve on their families and the Jewish community. The organized Jewish community, while lobbying to retain their refugee status, is preparing for the eventuality that they will be considered immigrants. Current fiscal pressures will exacerbate, causing additional strain on already stretched budgets.

Fiscal pressures in resettlement policy have created ethical dilemmas in regard to the allocation of scarce resources. A professional social worker of a local federation was clearly disturbed by the dilemmas his agency was facing.

The social worker's comments are examined from talmudic and ethical perspectives. The talmudic perspective concerns the biblical command to give to the poor "sufficient for his need." The ethical perspective encompasses the value of justice and the ethics of intimacy. The aim of this chapter is to demonstrate the interface between Judaic and professional values in the analysis of an ethical dilemma in Jewish communal service. The social worker raised these concerns in an interview.

> As you know, there has been a significant influx of Russian Jews to the United States. This has necessitated the raising and expenditure of more funds. In our federation we have not raised enough to cover the expenses of resettlement. There are more immigrants than we can handle, and their needs have outpaced our resources. We are caught in a serious dilemma of what to do in this situation.
>
> The first question of immediate concern is how much we should give, since resources are limited and there are other pressing needs in the community. This is an emergency, as the Russians come with very little, but there are other priorities too. For example, should we reduce allocations to Jewish education in order to support resettlement of Russian Jews?

PRINCIPLE OF *TZEDAKAH*

The allocation of scarce resources is not a new problem. The sages of the Talmud were puzzled by the meaning of "sufficient" in the biblical command: "But you shall surely open your hand unto him and lend him sufficient for his need in that which he lacks" (Deuteronomy. 15:8). How much is sufficient, and how is it to be determined? Are there any guidelines?

> Our rabbis taught: "Sufficient for his need" implies that you are commanded to maintain him, but you are not commanded to make him rich; "in that which he lacks" includes even a horse to ride upon and a slave to run before him. It was related about Hillel the Elder that he bought for a certain poor man who was of a good

family a horse to ride upon and a slave to run before him. On one occasion he could not find a slave to run before him, so he himself ran before him for three miles.

(Talmud Ketubot 67b)

The Talmud's answer is based on the principle of *tzedakah* (justice). The sages set a minimum standard beyond which the donor is not obliged to go. One must maintain the poor according to their previously accustomed life-style, but not excessively. Hillel applied this principle to the poor man of a good family. Since the man was accustomed to ride on a horse and to be attended by a slave, Hillel supplied these domestic accoutrements when he could no longer afford to do so.

Can this principle and its case illustration serve as a guide for the resettlement of Jews from the former Soviet Union in the United States? If we were to apply it as Hillel did, we would be obliged as a community to provide these new immigrants with the same necessities and comforts they had before they emigrated. These include a place to live, a job, education for their children, vocational training, and the ability to speak the language (i.e., English as a second language)—in effect, all the services that are currently being provided.

As the influx continues, funds allocated for resettlement are being depleted. Although they have been attempting to follow Hillel's example, many communities can no longer afford to do so. Is it right to limit services to this group when funds are scarce? Is there talmudic sanction for a policy of communal resistance? Resistance may be inferred from the second interpretation of "sufficient for his need."

Our rabbis taught: It once happened that the people of Upper Galilee bought for a poor member of a good family of Sepphoris a pound of meat every day. "A pound of meat! What is the greatness in this?" R. Huna replied: "It was a pound of fowl's meat. And if you prefer, I might say: They purchased ordinary meat for a pound of money." R. Ashi replied: "The place was a small village, and every day a beast had to be spoiled for his sake" [all the meat that remained after his one pound had been taken off had to be thrown away for lack of buyers and consumers].

(Talmud Ketubot 67a)

In the stories, Hillel and the villagers made great sacrifices in order to accommodate the former life-style of the poor men. Though the villagers were themselves poor, they felt it was incumbent upon them to do so. However, there is a sense of compulsion in the phrase "a beast *had* to be spoiled for his sake." The villagers could not afford to slaughter these animals, but they did so for the sake of the mitzvah. This story introduces the concept of donor resistance in the act of *tzedakah*.

Resistance appears to be an underlying theme in the social worker's delineation of the ethical dilemma. The federation would like to serve every Jew from the former Soviet Union who comes to the community but it cannot, because serious cuts that the community is not ready to support would have to be made in other services.

THE MORAL CLAIMS OF RECIPIENTS

The focus thus far has been on the donor's responsibilities to recipients. Do recipients have any moral claims on donors' benevolence; are they justified in asking for services? Moral claims would obligate the community to respond. Moral claims are based on the value of justice, which according to Levy (1974a, p. 43), includes

> efforts to ensure equal opportunities and protection to all persons within the framework of formal and informal institutions and practices. . . . The social worker who engages in advocacy at the justice level, whether on behalf of individual clients or of classes of persons to whom he feels a professional obligation, devotes himself to effecting for them the rights and entitlements legally and socially available to others.

When emigration of Jews from the former Soviet Union was only a trickle, and the "refusenik" movement was gaining momentum, the value of justice undergirded appeals by the United States government and the organized Jewish community to the Soviet government that emigration quotas be eliminated. Protest marches and rallies also stressed justice and the humane treatment of Jews in the Soviet Union. These immigrants expect rights and entitlements available to others based on the Jewish value of *tzedakah* and the American value of justice.

Corrective justice "involves the selective consideration of the needs of deprived groups and the institution of deferential provisions for them in light of their present condition and past deprivation" (Levy 1974a, p. 43). Corrective justice is not merely a case of ensuring equal access to goods and services, but giving certain groups and individuals special preferences. It is an effort to redress grievances and compensate for past inequities.

Corrective justice supports the preferential treatment of Jews from the former Soviet Union through the allocation of special funds. It suggests that they not be compared with other groups; that they are special because of their history of harassment, discrimination, and persecution. Corrective justice demands the unequal distribution of resources in favor of the aggrieved group. As a consequence, it may penalize others who are also vulnerable and who deserve community services.

ETHICAL CONFLICT

The ethical conflict in social planning for Jews from the former Soviet Union is located in Jewish values and social work values. Federation, representing the Jewish community, bases its resettlement policy on the Jewish values of *tzedakah, hesed* (loving-kindness), *pidyon sh'vuyim* (the redemption of captives), and *hachnassat orchim* (welcoming guests into one's home). The social worker's values are belief in human dignity, care for the needy, nondiscrimination, and social justice. Since values imply ethical obligations, federation owes Russian Jewish immigrants a range of services based upon its Jewish and professional values.

These values also support services to other groups in the Jewish community. The vulnerability of children, single parents, the elderly, and the sick confirms their moral claims for services. Their claims and those of the immigrants are based upon the same set of values. As is typical of ethical dilemmas, the choice is "between two 'rights' and two 'goods' that possess equal weight and importance" (Linzer 1989, p. 183).

The ethical dilemma is: how should scarce funds be distributed? Should funds be shifted from current recipients to the immigrants or not? The dilemma appears to be equally balanced between the claims of immigrants and the claims of local residents. However, immigrant advocates base their moral claim for preferential treatment not only on the value of justice but on the value of corrective justice. They argue that this group should receive more services in order to redress past inequities. They buttress their arguments with the Jewish value of *pidyon sh'vuyim,* which takes precedence over supporting the poor and building a synagogue; there is no greater mitzvah (Maimonides, *Mishneh Torah,* Laws of Gifts to the Poor 8:10–11).

It is in the nature of advocacy that it presupposes forces that resist the advocate's initiative. Some groups in the Jewish community insist that Jews from the former Soviet Union settle in Israel. This position coincides with the official policy of the government of Israel that Israel is the Jewish homeland, and that it needs their knowledge and experience to help build the state. According to this view, the Jewish community does not ethically owe the Russian Jews any preferential treatment, and therefore it is not so readily apparent that their moral claims for service take primacy over those of other groups.

RESPONSIBILITY OF RECIPIENTS

The flip side of Russian Jews' moral claims is whether they have an obligation to lower their expectations of the Jewish community. Can they legitimately claim entitlements commensurate with their former living conditions, or must they reduce these claims because of the community's fiscal constraints? These questions are implied in two subsequent talmudic stories.

> A certain man once applied to R. Nehemiah [for maintenance]. "What do your meals consist of?" [the rabbi] asked him. "Of fat meat and old wine," the other replied. "Will you consent [the rabbi asked him] to live with me on lentils?" [The other consented,] lived with him on lentils and died. "Alas," [the rabbi] said, "for this man whom Nehemiah has killed." On the contrary, he should [have said], "Alas for Nehemiah, who killed this man!" [The fact,] however, [is that the man himself was to blame, for] he should not have cultivated his luxurious habits to such an extent.
>
> (Talmud Ketubot 67b)

In this story, Rabbi Nehemiah does not go out of his way to supply the poor man with his normal diet, as Hillel would have done.

He is content to share his plain meals with him. When the man dies, the sages deliberate on placing blame. The first view is that Rabbi Nehemiah was responsible because he changed the man's diet so abruptly, and the man is pitied. The second view is that Rabbi Nehemiah is pitied because he caused the man's death. The conclusion is that the man was to blame for his own death because he cultivated excessively luxurious habits. The poor person should have reduced his expectations of the community's largesse. For the first time in its discussion of "sufficient," the Talmud holds the poor responsible for circumscribing their demands.

The next story concludes differently.

> A man once applied to Raba [for maintenance]. "What do your meals consist of?" he asked him. "Of fat chicken and old wine," the other replied. "Did you not consider," [Raba] asked him, "the burden of the community?" "Do I," the other replied, "eat of theirs? I eat [the food] of the All-Merciful; for we have learned: 'The eyes of all wait for Thee, and Thou givest them their food in due season' (Psalms 145:15); this, since it is not said 'in their season' but 'in his season,' teaches that the Holy One, blessed be He, provides for every individual his food in accordance with his own habits." Meanwhile, there arrived Raba's sister, who had not seen him for thirteen years, and brought him a fat chicken and old wine. "What a remarkable incident!" [Raba exclaimed; and then] he said to him, "I apologize to you, come and eat."
>
> (Talmud Ketubot 67b)

By asking the poor man to consider the burden of the community, Raba declared that Jewish communal funds were not unlimited, and excessive expenditures for one person would deplete the resources for others. The man, however, was somewhat of a sage himself. In answering Raba, he cited the theological source for the mitzvah of *tzedakah:* God's ultimate ownership of all wealth and possessions, and His provision for all people. Donors are intermediaries between God and recipients; they are not expending their own funds but are merely caretakers of God's property. The arrival of Raba's sister and the coincidence of her gift seemed to vindicate the man's argument. Raba's apology followed.

This story reflects the tension between two formidable moral claims: the needs of the community versus the needs of the individual. When they clash, whose needs are paramount, and in which circumstances? Does one have any moral responsibility to defer to the other? Since funds are always inadequate to meet all of a community's needs, how should priorities be determined? How much is enough, and how much is not enough? Are there any guidelines for drawing the line between "maintaining" an individual, a group, a service, and not making them "rich"? The difficulty in answering these questions is reflected in the four talmudic stories that attempt to explain the verse "sufficient for his need is that which he lacks."

Each story presents a different approach to the issue. By invoking the principle of maintaining the poor and not making him rich, the sages, in effect, endorsed parameters on individual and communal philanthropic expenditures. Giving *tzedakah* is not unlimited. Yet, it is in the nature of principles that they merely guide and do not specifically prescribe. Each ethically ambiguous situation is different, and the principle, though it cannot resolve, can contribute to the analysis. The variety of the talmudic stories illustrates the complexity of applying the principle. In the code of Jewish law, Hillel's action is preferred, but the recipient has a moral responsibility to reduce demands. When studied in depth, the stories reveal a rich repository of rabbinic thought on a complex moral and ethical issue. They inspire professionals to apply them creatively to the allocation of scarce resources for immigrants from the former Soviet Union and other countries.

RESOLUTION OF THE ETHICAL DILEMMA

The ethical dilemma was understood to be between the needs of the community and the needs of the individual/group, with the necessity of choosing one over the other. However, this option is neither tenable nor feasible. Analogously, so long as the abortion debate is framed solely as between the pro-choicers and the pro-lifers, there will be no possibility of conflict resolution. Conflict cannot be resolved when absolute principles are invoked. Toulmin (1981, p. 34) argues that "moral wisdom is exercised not by those who stick to a single principle come what may, absolutely and without exception, but rather by those who understand that, in the long run, no principle, however absolute, can avoid running up against another equally absolute principle."

When applying principles to ethics, Toulmin distinguishes between families and strangers. There are differences between moral relations with our families, intimates, neighbors, and associates and with complete strangers. In dealing with intimates, such as spouses, children, friends, and close colleagues, we expect to make allowances for their individual personalities and tastes. In dealing with strangers, such as the bus driver, the hotel barber, or the movie ticket taker, there may be no basis for making allowances and no chance for doing so. In transient encounters our moral obligations are limited and mainly negative, i.e., to avoid acting in an offensive manner. "So, in the ethics of strangers, respect for rules is all, and the opportunities for discretion are few. In the ethics of intimacy, discretion is all, and the relevance of strict rules is minimal" (Toulmin 1981, p. 35).

It is readily apparent that former Soviet Jews are not in the category of strangers but intimates; they are fellow Jews, members of the Jewish extended family, to whom the ethics of discretion should be applied. Given the shortfall in fund-raising campaigns, may federations tell the immigrants that they are not welcome? Is it right to say to a family member, "we have no room for you"? Morally, we cannot turn away our family from services. This implies that federations must either meet all the immigrants' needs or exclude newcomers after the saturation point has been reached.

The ethics of intimacy suggests a more modified approach guided by discretion and the avoidance of confrontation. The search for compromise, informed by the talmudic principle of maintenance, has enabled federations to implement several significant cost-saving policies and practices. Volunteers have been enlisted to help the immigrants find jobs. Because of the amount of time involved in finding jobs and their scarcity in many fields, immigrants have been urged to accept their first job offers. Only first-degree relatives, such as parents, children, brothers, and sisters, but no cousins, have been accepted for absorption into some communities. In many communities, family-reunification programs have been instituted whereby relatives of new immigrants assist in financing their resettlement. These are considered to be realistic compromises between accepting or rejecting all newcomers.

Issues that are still being debated include whether federations should continue to provide cash grants or loans to be repaid by the families. As to a preference between loans and grants, the Talmud frames the issue in this way:

> Our rabbis taught: If a man has no means and does not wish to be maintained out of the poor funds, he should be granted the sum he requires as a loan and then it can be presented to him as a gift; so R. Meir. The sages, however, said: "It is given to him as a gift and then it is granted to him as a loan." "As a gift? He surely refuses to take gifts!" Raba replied: "It is offered to him in the first instance as a gift."
>
> (Talmud Ketubot 67b)

As the opinion favors the sages, the funds and services are to be offered first as a gift and then as a loan. A gift does not enhance the recipient's dignity, whereas a loan does.

Federations can be guided by this talmudic discussion. A difference might be made between services and cash grants, where services are offered as a "gift" and cash as a "loan." At this time, both cash and services are given as gifts to immigrants. However, if refugee status is rescinded, and the government ceases to allocate funds, then the Jewish community would have to consider eliminating cash grants and providing services only. Families would have to guarantee financial support.

CONCLUSION

Resettlement policies for Jews from the former Soviet Union are still evolving. The community's moral struggle to act with sensitivity to the plight of the immigrants and to meet its fiscal obligations to other residents is in the finest Jewish traditions of *tzedakah, hesed,* and *pidyon sh'vuyim.* Soviet Jewry advocates, guided by the mitzvah of *pidyon sh'vuyim,* have argued for a hierarchy of priorities which has actually resulted in reductions in local services. In determining the allocation of scarce resources, both lay and professional leaders can illuminate difficult choices through the interface of ancient Judaic texts and traditions with modern professional values and fiscal realities.

Chapter 12

Ethical Dilemmas in the Jewish Community Center

This chapter presents an historical overview of major trends and ideological issues in the Jewish community center field, followed by five ethical dilemmas.

AN HISTORICAL GLANCE

Jewish communal institutions, particularly the Jewish community center, have gone through three phases in relation to Jewish values. They are now in the midst of the fourth phase, where the rationale for sectarian services is being heavily based on the Jewish heritage.

The first period, from 1850 to 1910, was marked by the large number of European Jews who brought with them Jewish values, traditions, and institutions from the shtetl. The second stage, 1910 to 1950, was characterized by the second generation, who avidly adopted American culture, and often discarded the traditions of their parents (Batshaw 1961). The third period, from 1950 to 1970, is the generation of the grandchildren and great-grandchildren of European immigrants, who demonstrated a tendency to recall their origins and plumb the values and traditions of the Jewish people.

The fourth period, 1970 to the present, has witnessed an erosion of the traditional institutions of Jewish life—Jewish marriage, family, education, synagogue affiliation, and ritual. The organized Jewish community is fighting an uphill battle to contain and reverse these trends.

These four periods mirror phases in the development of Jewish social services and particularly the Jewish community center.

At first, Jewish immigrants organized, on a voluntary basis, literary societies for recreation, landsmanschaften for mutual help, and synagogues for spiritual needs. In the centers, the immigrants studied literature, learned the English language, and discussed common issues. It was the period of the Americanization of the Jewish immigrant.

In the second period, professional knowledge about individual and group behavior and community organization was developed. The Jewish community adopted the knowledge and skills offered by social workers whose goals in Jewish centers were personality and community development. This period enabled the children of the immigrants to professionalize their agencies in order to meet their acculturation needs in American society. Center services were secularized and not related to Jewish values.

During the third period, which began with the Janowsky report (1948), emphasis was placed on defining the "Jewish" in Jewish community centers. Efforts were devoted to articulating the philosophy and programs of "Jewish content" in Jewish community centers in conjunction with professional social work methods. Until recently, social group work was the host method in centers, and its philosophy, methods, and skills were utilized to achieve the center's purposes (Linzer 1964). In a study of social work and the Jewish community center, Levy (1976c) found that the values which tended to guide practitioners were frequently seen by them as influences of their social work ideology.

As centers expanded their services, other professions found a niche. Jewish culture specialists, Jewish educators, physical education workers, early-childhood educators, and business administrators dissipated the central role previously played by social workers. In the fourth period, since the 1970s, social work has been in the minority compared with the other combined professions. The small friendship clubs of earlier eras that required the ministration of social workers hardly exist. The role of social work in centers has diminished, creating opportunities for other disciplines.

The delimitation of social work paralleled the development of the Jewish communal professional, an all-encompassing identity that center and other agency professionals could adopt, despite their particular professional orientations. By offering an M.A. in Jewish communal service, some graduate schools have tried to professionalize Jewish communal work, and have competed with social work and other professionals in Jewish communal service (Bubis et al., 1985). In the 1970s, competent and highly skilled people in different professions entered the center field. This trend has persisted in the 1980s and 1990s.

The diversity of professional staff is not the only major development that has taken place in the center field. The Jewish Community Centers Association's study on Jewish education (Jewish Welfare Board 1984), the final report of the Task Force on Reinforcing the Effectiveness of Jewish Education in the JCC (Jewish Community Centers Association 1995), and the book, Jewish Education and the Jewish Community Center (Chazan and Charendoff 1994) have boldly reemphasized and expanded the central theme of the Janowsky report, that the Jewish center should be a vehicle of Jewish identification by becoming a Jewish educational institution. Ideologies abound. Dubin (1986) offered multifaceted conceptions of Jewish content in the center, Chazan (1987) presented a Jewish educational philosophy for centers, and Rosen (1985) viewed Jewish cultural arts as the fulfillment of Jewish educational goals.

There is a disparity between the center's Jewish goals and members' reasons for joining. Though centers have moved into more formal Jewish education with the hiring of Jewish educators, people do not generally join centers for their Jewish programming. They join for early-childhood services, physical education activities, the health club, cultural activities, and camping, among others. They view the center as a means of affiliating with Jewish life and belonging to the Jewish community. Though this has not translated into attending Jewish educational activities, attendance will increase as the idea catches on and the need to learn about the Jewish heritage becomes more prominent.

THE CENTER'S IDEOLOGY

Though the role of social work has diminished in practice, it still retains a prominent place in the center's ideology. Excerpts from the Code of Ethics of the Association of Jewish Center Professionals (1984) place social work goals first in individual and group betterment.

> The Association of Jewish Center Professionals is committed to helping individuals and groups develop to their fullest capacities, to affirm and interpret the enduring values of Jewish tradition, and to make a positive contribution to the greater community of which they are a part.

Social work ideology can be discerned in the priority of ethical responsibility:

> I regard as my primary obligation the welfare of the people being served. This obligation imposes upon me the necessity of working to improve social conditions, the quality of life, and assure Jewish continuity.
>
> I respect the human rights of the persons I serve or employ.
>
> I am committed to a concept of Judaism based on Jewish ethics, morals, culture, history, tradition and values.

The welfare of the people being served, the development of their fullest capacities, and the improvement of social conditions attest to the social work goals of the center field. The promotion of Jewish values and the assurance of Jewish continuity attest to its Jewish goals. The Jewish goals have been receiving greater attention because of the erosion of Jewish life due to assimilation and intermarriage.

The Model Code of Ethics of the Conference of Jewish Communal Service (1984) stresses the priority of Jewish goals over social work goals: "Professional/communal practice in the Jewish community is based upon Jewish values, humanitarian consideration, democratic ideas and professional knowledge and skill." The primacy of ethical responsibility is toward the Jewish people.

> I regard as primary my obligation to the continuity, well-being, and survival of the Jewish people and to the welfare of the Jewish community, its organization and individuals.
>
> I am committed to a concept of Judaism based on Jewish ethics.
>
> I recognize the special relationship between Israel and Jewish Diaspora.
>
> I support the principle that Jewish communal service requires appropriate professional training and continuing education.

The Association of Center Professionals, established by social workers, emphasizes the social work values of personality development and community welfare. The Conference of Jewish Communal Service, the umbrella organization of all Jewish communal agencies, represents a diverse group of professionals that includes social workers, Jewish educators, vocational counselors, synagogue administrators, camping specialists, and community relations professionals. It stresses the Jewish purposes that unite them rather than the distinct professional purposes that may divide them.

The dual emphasis of the ethical responsibilities of professionals in Jewish community centers—personality development and Jewish continuity—reflect centers' dual commitment to social work values and ethics as well as Jewish values and ethics. The potential for conflict is rife when these two systems of thought are juxtaposed. Four cases illustrate the conflicts that arise from dual commitments.

SERVING THE COGNITIVELY IMPAIRED ON THE SABBATH

When we started our service to the cognitively impaired, we had a Monday night program for moderately impaired adults and a Friday night program for severely impaired adults. We decided that the program for the severely impaired would be on Friday evening because it had to be experiential, and not didactic, and the best way to do that was through an experience of Shabbat.

In order for this program to exist, individuals would have to be transported. The Orthodox community was strongly opposed. We informed them that we would offer them a program on another night. But we never received a response to this offer. Most of the impaired Orthodox were living in non-denominational group homes run by secular agencies and Catholic Charities. They were not going to attend Shabbat services. It was never a problem for the population itself.

We offered to initiate a program for people who were within walking distance of the synagogue. We even suggested a buddy system where a member of the synagogue would pick someone up from his home and walk with him on Friday nights and Saturday mornings. Nobody ever picked up on that either. We made ourselves available to serve the Orthodox impaired community, but we didn't find them because they were probably being served by group homes.

Resolution. It was our choice to proceed. We recognized there are many Jews who ride on the Sabbath and who observe it in many different ways. As long as this part of the community wanted the service, we felt an obligation to bring them back into the community.

Ultimately, we decided that we would have a program on Wednesday evenings for the severely impaired as well. It has never been as good as the program on Friday nights. I truly believe that I was right, that programmatically the Sabbath is the best way to experience the celebration of Jewishness.

Discussion

This issue touches upon Jewish law, its pluralistic interpretation in modern times, the role of the center as a Jewish institution serving the Jewish community, the social work philosophy that undergirds its group services, and the needs of the group being served.

The Sabbath is one of the pillars of Judaism. It attests to the belief in God as the creator of the world (Exodus 20:7–10) and as the God of history (Deuteronomy 5:11–14). It is a constant reminder of the spiritual brought into relation with the material, of the Jew's relinquishing control over nature to the creator of nature (Grunfeld 1956). On one day a week, Jews turn away from mundane concerns to sublime thoughts, from matter to spirit, from worries to relaxation. Heschel (1951, p. 29) described this "turning away" process eloquently:

> In the tempestuous ocean of time and toil there are islands of stillness where man may enter a harbor and reclaim his dignity. The island is the seventh day, the Sabbath, a day of detachment from things, instruments and practical affairs as well as of attachment to the spirit.

Ahad Ha-am captured the Sabbath's significance for Jews in his pithy statement: "More than Israel has kept the Sabbath, the Sabbath has kept Israel" (cited in Millgram 1965, p. 253).

The laws of the Sabbath are varied, complex, and far-reaching. The thirty-nine major categories of prohibited work and their extensive offshoots derive from the juxtaposition of Sabbath observance with the building of the Temple (Exodus 35:1–21). Among them are such prohibitions as kindling a fire, writing, building, and carrying a burden from one place to another (Grunfeld 1956). The Talmud, Maimonides' Mishneh Torah, and the Code of Jewish Law (Shulhan Arukh) are the major sources of the interpretation, application, and codification of the Sabbath laws. Questions regarding Sabbath observance that arose in the course of centuries that were not codified in these books were directed at leading rabbis of the day. Their responses comprise an extensive literature that addressed the observance of the Sabbath along with other mitzvot in conjunction with the technology of the times (Feldman 1968, pp. 3–18).

Pluralistic interpretations of the Sabbath laws arose in modern times, particularly over the use of electricity and driving a car. The Orthodox maintain that the Torah's prohibition against kindling a fire on the Sabbath (Exodus 35:3) extends to electricity and driving. Conservatives prohibit driving a car except for attending services in the temple. Reform Jews do not consider the Torah's Sabbath injunctions applicable to modern times; instead, the positive observances are stressed (Millgram 1965). Because of pluralistic interpretations of Jewish law, institutions and individuals decide on their own how they want to observe the Sabbath, and what forms their activities will take.

THE ROLE OF THE CENTER

The center has never been ideologically identified with a Jewish religious movement. It is not a religious institution, but one that strives to create a "secular Jewish culture" (Sklare 1971). This does not mean that religious elements do not have a place in the center's policies and programs. For example, many centers maintain a kashrut policy. While variations of this policy abound, it is widespread, not because the center is obligated to uphold Torah law, but because of a fundamental principle that undergirds all its services: every Jew should be able to partake of food served at center activities, and should not feel rejected because it is not kosher.

Since each center is autonomous, the complexion of its Jewish practices varies, depending on the influence of the local community. In a community where the Orthodox are active members of the center and its board, the likelihood is that halakhic practices would be more pervasive in the center than in a community dominated by Conservative, Reform, or Reconstructionist Jews.

During the 1960s, in the debate about opening centers on the Sabbath (Linzer 1963), rabbis across the religious spectrum were opposed because it would detract from Sabbath attendance at their synagogues. Some were concerned about hillul shabbat, the profanation of the Sabbath that would occur due to the weekday activities taking place in the center. Others felt that Jews would have to drive to the center, thus constituting a violation of the Sabbath.

Solender (1962, p. 44) has written:

> Such matters as the Sabbath practices of Centers are local community problems which must be dealt with by the local community. They are issues around which there are an infinite variety of views, even within the religious community. JWB as the national body of the Centers has reaffirmed the original recommendation of the Janowsky report that Centers should be open on the Sabbath only for those activities which are in consonance with the day. JWB has urged that determination of a given Center's policy within this framework should be made with the fullest consultation with all affected local groups.

For years, centers were closed on the Sabbath and holidays. Gradually, communities introduced compromises. In some, the center is completely closed; in others, it is closed only during the times of synagogue services. When it is open on Saturday afternoons, it attempts to offer activities in the spirit of the Sabbath. In some centers this includes physical education, while in others it does not. Centers that provide Oneg Shabbat programs on Friday evenings point out that they are providing Sabbath enrichment for people who do not normally attend synagogue services.

In deciding to serve Jewish cognitively impaired members on Friday evenings, the center claims that this group ordinarily does not attend Sabbath services and, in fact, is served by secular agencies and Catholic Charities. The center believes it is enhancing this group's Jewish identity by providing a Sabbath experience.

The Orthodox concur with the ends but disagree with the means. The group's traveling to the center on the Sabbath constitutes a violation of Sabbath law. Though the center does not view itself as an Orthodox institution committed to uphold Jewish law, as a Jewish communal institution it has a mandate to serve the entire Jewish community. This center insisted that the Jewish needs of the cognitively impaired should be served, and the Sabbath is one of the means for achieving this goal.

CONFLICTING VALUES

One of the center's primary values is service to the entire Jewish community. The center is a community-based institution, supported by the Jewish federation and public funding, as well as by the program fees and membership dues of an ideologically diverse spectrum of Jews.

Another center value is pluralism. The center rejects a monolithic approach to Jewish life and believes that there are many ways to express one's Judaism. It is the one institution in Jewish life where Jews of all religious and ideological persuasions can join together to forge a united community.

Because it maintains an ideology of pluralism, the center does not take a halakhic stance on any religious matter, particularly on issues where there are differences among the rabbis in the community. Representing the spectrum of Jewish life, the center attempts to meet diverse community needs, though they may not be sanctioned by all segments of the Jewish community.

A third value is the primacy of the client (National Association of Social Workers 1980). Social workers in centers, guided by professional values, provide services to vulnerable populations where professional knowledge and skills are required. The needs of the cognitively impaired are not only social but Jewish. As the social worker's primary responsibility, the group should be afforded opportunities to participate in programs that strengthen their Jewish identity, even as the center helps other Jewish groups to achieve this goal.

A contrary value is represented by the Orthodox rabbis' argument that the center should uphold the sanctity of the Sabbath.

Though the center is not a religious institution, it should not adopt policies or sponsor activities that offend an important segment of the community.

CONFLICTING ETHICAL STANCES

Since ethics is based on values, the center staff would be acting ethically if it sponsored Sabbath activities for the cognitively impaired because of the center's values of community, pluralism, and primacy of client needs. The decision appears to be consistent with ethical principles and deontological and consequentialist theories.

Deontologists espouse an action to be right if it is inherently right and consistent with values and ethical principles. Having established a relationship with the group through prior services, the center is required to provide a Jewish experience by the principle of fidelity. The center staff has determined that the Oneg Shabbat is beneficial because it strengthens the members' Jewish identity. The decision is ethically consistent with consequentialist theory because it leads to good consequences (Binkly 1961), strengthening the members' Jewish identity.

On the negative side, the Orthodox would argue that a decision that violates Jewish law cannot be deontologically right, nor lead to good consequences. According to Jewish law, a mitzvah that is fulfilled through a wrongful act (*mitzvah haba'a ba'averah*) is invalid. Sponsoring a program that violates the Sabbath is unethical because it causes the group to override Jewish values.

Resolution. The center's professional staff resolved the conflict by proceeding with the program. This was consistent with the center's values and ethics as a communal institution that serves all segments of the Jewish community. There was no intention to offend the Orthodox, only to help a group of handicapped Jews to experience their Jewishness more deeply.

CENTER POLICIES ON SABBATH, HOLIDAYS, AND KASHRUT

The center that serves cognitively impaired Jews on the Sabbath is part of a trend of opening centers on the Sabbath. Economics seem to be the driving force.

With federations cutting their allotments, centers are engaging in more fund-raising efforts. As centers embark on elaborate marketing programs to increase membership, they attract the non-Jewish population, and begin to depend on them for income. Non-Jews are attracted to centers because of the high quality of their programs and services. As with Jews, non-Jews see the center as a place to spend their leisure time on weekdays and Saturdays, particularly in the health and fitness center. Along with many Jews, they claim that they do not observe the Sabbath and should not be deprived of the use of the center's facilities.

A similar plaint against centers being closed is heard from Reform Jews who do not observe the second day of Jewish holidays and instead return to work. Since they normally obtain day-care services for their children at the centers, they insist that the day-care also be available on the second festival days.

A third example involves thrift shops operated by centers in order to augment income. Since the Sabbath is the most lucrative day for doing business, centers want to keep the shop open.

Why is the sanctity of the Sabbath being chipped away? The Sabbath has lost its luster because Jews are highly assimilated to the values of the larger society, and do not want their personal freedom constricted.

How should requests for opening centers on the Sabbath be handled? There is no panacea. As each community is unique in its Jewish constellation, it will have to determine the balance of benefit over deficit in operating the center on the Sabbath. Driven by the need for economic viability, centers will continue to acquiesce to the requests and demands of their constituents to open their facilities on the Sabbath and holidays. These holy days will not be discernibly different from the secular weekdays. Centers will have lost an opportunity to educate their members on the meaning and sanctity of these days. What the center may gain in income it may lose in failing to preserve the sacred in Jewish life.

There is a paradox in center policy. Centers try to combat the erosion of Jewish life by teaching members the values and traditions of Judaism, while opening the building on Sabbaths and holidays for an array of activities to accommodate the recreational and social needs of their members. Centers are permitting economics to compromise their Jewish mission.

The erosion of kashrut policies in centers seems to be evident. A strict kashrut policy affords all Jews the opportunity to partake of food served at center functions without feeling left out. Centers have exerted extra effort and expense to maintain kosher kitchens and caterers. These standards appear to be evaporating due to fiscal constraints. Centers are renting out their kitchens and day camp sites to non-Jewish organizations that bring in less expensive non-kosher caterers. Although this is rationalized as a mere rental arrangement, the event takes place under the centers' auspices, and is seen as legitimate. It is apparent that centers are permitting economics to compromise their Jewish mission.

TEEN BASKETBALL ON THE SABBATH

Another ethical dilemma involving Sabbath policy in the Jewish community center arose when teen basketball-league games were scheduled to be played on the Sabbath.

We bring into the Y a very large population of Jewish teens through basketball. We play against other Y's and temples, and Catholic organizations. Gym scheduling is very tough for all the agencies during the week because the teens do school work, attend Hebrew high school and afterschool programs.

Saturday is a day that agencies can get gym time, so league games are scheduled on that day. I had to make a decision: do I want to participate in a league that plays on Saturdays? As a Jewish organization, we are not open on Saturdays and it is not within the religion's best interest to play ball on that day. On the other hand, sports is a major vehicle for attracting this age group to the Y. Through the league I can get them involved in teen council, clothing drives, Purim Carnival, etc.

My dilemma is: do we withdraw from the league because of the Sabbath policy, do I take forfeits for some of the games that would be played on Saturdays, or do I decide to let them play on Saturdays? How do I meet my commitment to my agency's Sabbath policy and, at the same time, meet my professional goals in maintaining the teens' interest in playing basketball? The problem is exacerbated because the teens themselves have no qualms about participating in the league on Saturdays.

The Y's Sabbath policy is consistent. If we take a weekend trip, we always make sure that we are there before sundown, that we are not driving during the Sabbath. The teen program in the building on Saturday evenings does not start until after sundown. From Friday at sundown until Saturday night we have no programs.

I am committed to the Y and its philosophy because I was helped by the Y as a teenager. If I didn't have this place to come to on Saturday nights I probably would have been on the street. The other goal for this age group is to keep these teens out of trouble by giving them a safe environment.

Resolution. We did not play on Saturdays. The building, which was never open on Sunday evenings, is now open for the league. On the away trips, we totally avoid Saturdays. Agency policy was deemed to be more important. The incentive for teens' staying on the team was to receive safe transportation to and from the building. We spoke to them about the meaning of the Sabbath and the Y as a Jewish organization. We felt it was important to respect not traveling on the Sabbath. I was able to respect agency policy as a professional and to find a workable solution.

No games were forfeited because I was able to offer Sunday slots and we picked up more games at home. That eliminated the need to go to other places on Saturday.

The new policy added time to our normal working hours. We also increased expenses by opening the building and hiring referees. The added financial expense paid off because the teens started to participate in other programs.

From this experience I learned that you have to decide what your priorities are and to eliminate the negative choices in order come up with a solution.

Discussion

As Solender (1962) has pointed out, each Jewish community center (JCC) or YM-YWHA (Y) reflects the community which it serves. The Y in the first case is open on the Sabbath. The Y in this case is closed, and is consistent in a policy that conforms with community values.

The Y's value conflict is readily apparent. Keeping the building closed expresses a commitment to uphold the holiness of the Sabbath and to promote the Y's role as an instrument of Jewish continuity.

The teenagers' needs are in stark opposition to Y policy. According to the respondent, they are more interested in playing basketball than in observing the Sabbath. In their view, playing in the league on Saturdays does not adversely affect their Jewish identity.

Despite knowledge of the group's values, the Y decided to reaffirm its Sabbath policy. It created a compromise solution that met the group's needs to play in the league, and its own goals of keeping them involved in Y activities and upholding its mission as a Jewish communal institution. The Y was willing to incur greater monetary expenses because advancing its Jewish purposes was a priority.

GROUP SERVICES FOR HOMOSEXUALS

Our guiding principle at the Y over the past few years has been that we should be open to all members of the Jewish community. We began with the easier populations, such as singles and the disabled. We developed programs for the cognitively impaired and learning disabled, the orthopedically handicapped, widows, widowers, divorcees and single parents—all kinds of family groups, including adopted children. We recently decided to serve Jewish alcoholics with Alcoholics Anonymous and Alanon groups. We feel that we should make it very clear that we are a community center for everyone.

Then we considered the homosexual group that is not recognized nor accepted by the organized Jewish community, although there is acceptance by some segments of the religious community. We serve them as individuals. But should we serve them in groups? What services should we provide? Should we try to change behavior? We would not run therapy groups because therapy is not our mission. A socialization group seemed to be totally out of the question.

Since this group is a large segment of the Jewish community, to deny it or to ignore it seems phony to us. The dilemma was, how do we serve this part of the community, while recognizing that there is a Jewish prohibition against their behavior? We discussed it quite a bit in a board-staff process. We obtained literature on the Jewish attitude toward homosexuality. Staff went to the gay synagogue and asked what kinds of services would be most helpful to them.

There has been no guidance by the federation and the Jewish Community Centers Association. It has been a totally ignored population that is screaming for recognition. According to Jewish law, we cannot recognize them; we cannot give communal dollars. No one has said that, but no one has said, "You are our sons and daughters and we are going to make you part of us. We hope and pray that you will change your ways, but we will accept you as you are, and you are part of us."

Resolution. We decided to offer a support group for the families of gays. We wanted to show that the Y is a place where these issues can be discussed within the Jewish community. It is not a great resolution, but we did recognize that this population exists.

Discussion

Homosexuality is an emotionally laden and controversial subject. It has achieved more notoriety in recent years due to the rapid spread of AIDS among the homosexual population. The respondent has touched upon the religious, ethical, and political ramifications of serving this group.

The Torah designates homosexual relations between males as sexual perversion (Leviticus 18:22) and threatens those who engage in such relations with capital punishment (Leviticus 20:13). Talmudic law extends the prohibition to lesbians. Jews are cautioned not to indulge in the abhorrent practices of the Egyptians and the Canaanites.

Rabbinic sources advance various reasons for the strict ban on homosexuality. It is an unnatural perversion that debases human dignity, frustrates the procreative purpose of sex, and damages family life. Jewish law rejects the view that homosexuality is to be regarded merely as a disease or morally neutral (Jakobovits 1972).

Lamm (1974, p. 204) suggests that homosexuality be regarded as pathology. "Judaism allows for no compromise in its abhorrence of sodomy, but encourages both compassion and efforts at rehabilitation." Lamm disapproves of gay synagogues but encourages congregations and other Jewish groups "to accord hospitality and membership, on an individual basis, to those 'visible' homosexuals who qualify for the category of the ill" (p. 205).

The Orthodox do not debate whether homosexuality is sinful, nor that those with physical and mental health needs should be served. "Nothing precludes, and everything supports, outreach to those involved in homosexual activity" (Freundel 1993).

Conservative Judaism adopted a resolution in 1991 that welcomes gays and lesbians as members in affiliated congregations (Rabbinical Assembly 1991). The Committee on Jewish Law and Standards affirmed that Conservative Judaism will not perform commitment ceremonies for gays and lesbians, and will not admit them to the cantorial or rabbinical schools. Authority is delegated to individual rabbis to permit gays and lesbians to serve as teachers, or to receive honors in the synagogue (Rabbinical Assembly 1992).

The Reform movement welcomes gays and lesbians into the rabbinate and as full members of synagogues. Gay synagogues affiliated with the Reform movement are granted equality with other Reform synagogues.

Reconstructionist Judaism views homosexuality as an alternative life-style, admits homosexuals to its rabbinical school, and advocates full equality in synagogue membership. Gay and lesbian synagogues are affiliated with this movement.

The religious movements' views of homosexuality are a function of their regard for the Torah's authority in modern times, and the degree of their acculturation to the larger society. As the gay rights movement gains political clout and legal recognition, homosexuals' demands for equality and acceptance within the religious Jewish community will increase.

While the religious movements have been discussing the ethics of gay rights and their inclusion into the religious community, major Jewish organizations have been rather silent. Few conferences have been held detailing the community's responsibilities to this group. The Y claims it has received no clear signals that would encourage the professional staff and board to take the step of offering group services to homosexuals.

Value Conflict

The ethical dilemma faced by the center in the case summarized above is based on a conflict of values. One of the primary values of the Jewish community center is to serve all members of the Jewish community without regard to age, gender, race, socioeconomic status, or sexual orientation. A second value stems from the center's social work orientation, which places primacy on the client and the client's needs. Both fundamental values ought to direct the staff to provide group services for homosexuals.

In contrast, the organized Jewish community has generally avoided this group and not reached out. The negative value may stem from the Torah's sanctions against the immoral behavior of homosexuals. Gays' and lesbians' needs are wrongfully devalued because their life-style is considered abhorrent. It is difficult for the center to counter this attitude of some segments of the Jewish community.

Ethical Dilemma

The ethical dilemma for the center is whether it is right not to serve gays and lesbians in groups. Since all other groups are served, why not these? The central value of the center—service to the entire Jewish community—should impel it to reach out to gays and lesbians, even as it does to alcoholics, the cognitively impaired, singles, etc. Deontologically it is the right thing to do. Consequentially, it may lead to good results as individuals gain support and acceptance in the group and develop a sense of belonging to the Jewish community.

It can also be argued that it is the wrong thing to do because homosexual behavior is deemed to be immoral in many circles, and the center should not support immorality. Moreover, serving this group may be construed as communal sanction of their behavior. The presence of AIDS among homosexuals makes them more susceptible to community ostracism, and raises ethical issues for professionals and caretakers (Hastings Center Report 1986).

Summary

The obligation to serve homosexuals as a group should have greater claim on the center staff because it is consistent with the center's dominant values of inclusiveness and nondiscrimination. Yet, the staff hesitated; they compromised by offering a group for the families of gays, but not for the gays themselves. The compromise could reflect the use of discretion in the ethics of intimacy, rather than adherence to absolute principles (Toulmin 1981). The staff could argue that Jewish homosexuals are in the category of intimates rather than strangers. They are center members, members of the Jewish people, the Jewish family writ large. They concluded that, even if the negative value demanded that they not be served as a distinct group, the ethics of discretion would at least permit their families to be served.

GAY COUPLES AS FAMILIES

Another related issue confronting centers occurs when a gay couple applies for a family membership. Gay couples as families have not been a category in center membership policy. Applications are being dealt with on an individual basis, with some centers acceding to their request.

This dilemma is similar to that of serving gays and lesbians in groups. Should they be considered families or not? According to Jewish tradition, they are not, but in modern times, they are gaining legal recognition as families. Which definition of family should the center adopt? By which values should it be guided—Jewish or secular or both? Even if the traditional Jewish definition denies their family status, would Jews of pluralistic religious persuasions agree? Need there be unanimous agreement in a definition of family to guide membership policy? Centers are wrestling with these questions because centers are nondenominational, inclusive of pluralistic ideologies, sensitive to Jewish traditional values but also to the needs of their constituents.

FUND-RAISING

It is axiomatic that centers may not engage in community-wide fund-raising campaigns due to a contractual agreement with federations. However, internal fund-raising is permitted in order to maintain the quality and quantity of center services.

> An executive director asked one of his department heads about the financial status of a center member for the purpose of determining the type of solicitation to make. Solicitations can be cash gifts, other assets, and planned giving and endowments. Planned giving could financially benefit the giver as well as the center.
> The department head felt it was unethical to disclose this information without the consent of the individual. Is this request ethical?

Discussion

The department head assumes that giving can be harmful, or at least resented by the potential donor; therefore, the information may not be revealed without the donor's consent. The Talmud calls this principle *ain chavin l'adam shelo b'fanav*—"one may not perform a detrimental act on behalf of a person without the person's consent."

When certain factors are considered, this situation can be turned into an advantage. Jews are in the forefront of giving tzedakah. It is a deeply held mitzvah that benefits the poor and indigent, the organized Jewish community, and the donor. The opposite talmudic principle may apply: *zachin l'adam shelo b'fanav*—"one may benefit a person not in his presence." By encouraging another to give tzedakah, one enables that person to do a mitzvah. Of the four types of donors to charity, the one who gives and wants others to give is designated as pious (Avot 5:16).

Individuals tend to give more support to institutions of which they are members than to those of which they are not. Support tends to increase when donors receive financial benefits in return. In the case of planned giving, the individual's benefits may be in the form of taxes and income. From a utilitarian perspective, the greater good will be served if the information is disclosed, the individual is approached, and a financial plan is devised.

CONCLUSION

The five cases discussed in this chapter illustrate the complexity of ethical decision-making when different value systems coalesce in the service situation. From the standpoint of the social work orientation to client needs, the center should offer programs to the cognitively disabled on Friday nights, to the teens on Saturday, to the gay population as a group, include gay couples as family members, and require informed consent from the potential donor.

From a Jewish perspective, the ethical imperative is not clear in many of the cases due to the ideological diversity in the Jewish community. The center's pluralistic orientation directs it from a unidimensional doctrinal observance of Jewish law toward a more inclusive neutral position. Because of the diverse values of their constituencies, centers' Sabbath, holiday, kashrut, and gay policies are fraught with conflicts. However, in approaching a potential donor to give tzedakah, there may be more unanimity.

With the cognitively impaired young adults and the teen basketball league, the centers took opposite stands on Sabbath policy; with serving gays as a group, the center compromised. Membership policy toward gay couples is still being deliberated. The executive director was convinced he was benefiting the potential donor and did not need his consent.

Jewish community centers are at a crossroads. Boards have become more businesslike, bottom-line oriented; staff represent a host of diverse professional disciplines; the members have become more demanding as they have developed a consumer orientation; and the forces of assimilation are more powerful than the defenses to thwart them.

The centers' mission is to strengthen Jewish communal life. However this is defined, centers have a difficult uphill battle to stem the forces of assimilation and meet the Jewish and personal needs of their diverse constituencies. They can succeed, for they are guided by their mission and the integration of professional and Jewish values.

Chapter 13

Autonomy versus Paternalism

The conflict between autonomy and paternalism pervades medical and health-care settings, but also emerges in the services to the elderly provided by YM-YWHAs and Jewish family services. In this dilemma, the professional's respect for the client's self-determination and autonomy sometimes clashes with the professional's paternalism and view of the client's best interests. The theoretical dimensions of this dilemma have been presented in chapter 2. They will now be applied to two cases of services to the elderly.

ELDERLY WIDOW IN DAUGHTER'S HOME

Day Care for the Elderly is a program for frail retirees who can no longer function in the traditional senior center and need medical monitoring, socialization, and case management. The program, co-sponsored by the YM-YWHA and the medical center, is operated by an interdisciplinary staff.

An 88-year-old Jewish widow had to move into her daughter's house because of increasing frailty. The daughter, separated from her husband, was only marginally able to cope with life and stress. Living with her was an 11-year-old son who had behavioral problems and learning disabilities.

Mrs. R moved into the home and attended the day center three days a week. We began to notice neglect of her medical care, as when she came in with a fracture and a few bruises on her scalp and legs. The family said she had lost her balance due to minimal stages of dementia. But when she came in with multiple bruises on her thighs and breasts, we suspected sexual abuse. The family claimed that the child was playing ball with grandma, and the marks and bruises were due to the ball hitting her body. The decision was made that this woman could not return to her home.

We called Protective Services and the police, and informed the family that we were not allowing the client to go back home. Our geriatrician wrote a letter of her findings and recommendations. We took the case to court. The client was placed in the hospital until a guardian could be assigned and nursing home placement arranged. The woman died in the hospital. We saw that as a blessing in disguise for her own safety because we feared that the daughter would continue to want to keep mom at home in order to receive her income.

This was an ethical dilemma because the client said she did not want anything to be done. Good social work practice respects a capable client's self-determination. However, through consultation with the physician and administration, the assessment was made that the client was not safe at home, that she was demented and incapable of making certain decisions herself. We felt we needed to make them for her, as this was a matter of life and death. We were united in the need to provide a safety haven for this individual.

Discussion

In chapter 2, the autonomy-paternalism dilemma was presented as a conflict between two values and principles. Autonomy is equivalent to self-determination, and paternalism is equivalent to agency responsibility. Neither self-determination nor agency responsibility is an absolute value that cannot be modified in a given situation.

The social work code of ethics places primacy on meeting client needs (National Association of Social Workers 1990), which implies support for client self-determination. However, self-determination is circumscribed when the client might harm others and/or himself. The agency then limits or overrides the client's decision, to prevent harm and promote welfare.

Though it is guided by the principle of respect for client autonomy, the agency is also guided by the principle of beneficence that requires the provision of services in the best interests of the client.

Most dilemmas for social workers and health care professionals involve conflicts between fostering client self-determination and promoting their best interests (Proctor et al. 1993).

In this case, support for the client's self-determination is weakened by her physical and mental condition, and her perceived incompetence. The agency felt a strong need to protect the client from physical abuse and possible death. There is considerable support for overriding self-determination and autonomy when life is perceived to be at stake (Reamer 1983b; Loewenberg and Dolgoff 1992).

The prima facie duty of nonmaleficence overrides other prima facie duties (Ross 1930). The principles of beneficence and non-maleficence combine to override the client's autonomy. While the decision appears to be paternalistic, it was not made to deliberately override the client's will but to protect her from abuse.

DECIDING FOR ALZHEIMER'S PATIENTS

The second case, by the same respondent, involves an elderly woman who refused to have a home-care attendant assist her with daily chores.

A bright, independent woman who has been coming to the YM-YWHA several days a week, was diagnosed with Alzheimer's. For the last year and a half, we have been suggesting that she hire someone to help her shop and cook, but she denies that she needs anyone. Denial is her survival kit in her deteriorating condition. The family has not told her that she has Alzheimer's because it would not be good for her to know. She has her own defense mechanism for her memory losses and her increased inability to care for herself. She is at risk because she lives alone, though the children visit and shop with her.

The son insists, and we concur, that she needs somebody to take care of her. The daughter says we have to have process because if we put somebody in without her approval she is going to sabotage. The practice issue is, how do I as a case manager help the family to deal with this situation? The ethical issue is whether to override her self-determination and place the attendant in the home.

I believe it is not right to send someone there against her wishes, thereby overruling her self- determination. This is different from the case of the 88-year-old frail woman who did not want to go to the hospital, because family support was nonexistent and she was more incompetent. This woman is more competent and her family is involved. These are significant variables in determining what is the right thing to do.

The woman was beginning to lose the ability to drive a car, but the family was unable to convince her not to. One day she drove to the hospital and crashed, and walked into doctor's office totally bruised. At that point, she made a decision not to drive a car any longer. For this client, something drastic had to happen for anything to be put into place. As of today there is going to be a home attendant for the first time. The family has talked with her, she has interviewed the individual, but does not recall. The dilemma was resolved through the involvement and agreement of all the parties.

Discussion

An ethical dilemma consists of a choice between two actions based on conflicting values. It can be resolved by assigning priority to one action and negating the other, but a price is paid. As Beauchamp and Childress (1989, p. 53) write:

> If a prima facie duty is outweighed or overridden, it does not simply disappear or evaporate. It leaves what Robert Nozick calls "moral traces." The agent should approach such a decision conscientiously and should expect to experience regret and perhaps even remorse at having to override and infringe this prima facie duty.

The professional felt "moral traces" when she overrode the first client's wish not to be placed in the hospital. She knew that she was denying the client's self-determination, but felt that the prima facie duty of nonmaleficence should prevail.

An ethical dilemma can also be resolved by applying a practice principle that integrates both ethical principles, thereby avoiding having to choose between them.

In the Alzheimer client case, the ethical principles are client autonomy and agency beneficence. Because the client was deemed somewhat competent, her autonomy was respected, and the agency's beneficence was not activated against her will. However, the agency and the children were still concerned with her ability to fend for herself, and monitored her movements closely.

The key event that resolved the dilemma was the car crash. By deciding to stop driving, the client admitted that she was incapable of maintaining the same degree of independent living as heretofore. The staff involved the entire family in a decision-making process to cope with the situation. This practice principle was effective in helping her to seek assistance with the tasks of daily life. By participating in the decision to have a home health aide, the client maintained a modicum of autonomy, the agency acted in a beneficent manner, and the ethical dilemma was resolved by the integration of both principles.

Additional tangential issues are evoked in this case. The degree to which the client may be a danger to herself will determine whether this is a practice or an ethical issue. If her life is threatened, there is no ethical dilemma about the need to protect her from harm. The practice issue revolves about the kinds of services to provide.

Providing a home health care attendant is complicated by the ethnic group to which this person belongs. Jewish elderly have been known to refuse the services of African-American and Hispanic care providers for cultural reasons. When client resistance confronts agency responsibility for the protection of life and well-being, the conflict is not easily resolved.

CONCLUSION

Two cases have been presented that illustrate the conflict between the ethical principles of autonomy and beneficence. In each case, it was not an arbitrary decision that resolved the dilemma, but a number of variables that gave weight to the resolution.

In the first case, the client's incompetence, abetted by the physical abuse to which she was being subjected, convinced the professional team that her life was more safe in the hospital than in her daughter's home. In the second case, the client's modicum of competence, pride, and independence, along with her family's cooperation with the agency, coalesced in the joint decision to accept a home health aide. Imposed decisions should be avoided when practice solutions may be found to justify a decision acceptable to the parties involved.

Chapter 14

Ethical Considerations in Serving Inter-married Couples

The National Jewish Population Survey found that a staggering 52 percent of Jews who married since 1985 wed persons who were not born or raised as Jews, and that only 6 percent of the non-Jewish spouses converted to Judaism (Council of Jewish Federations 1991). The data indicate an alarming increase in intermarriage rates over the last thirty-five years and the acceptance of intermarriage by large segments of the Jewish community. The organized Jewish community, alarmed at the magnitude of the problem, has taken steps to combat it. Federations have established Commissions on Continuity to develop programs to strengthen Jewish identity. Synagogues, Jewish community centers, Jewish family services, and Jewish schools are engaged in outreach and services to intermarried couples and their children.

This chapter analyzes ethical dilemmas in policies toward the intermarried that confronted two Jewish family service agencies. The dilemmas dealt with withholding information from a couple contemplating intermarriage, and serving the intermarried. Since ethics has been conceived as "values in action" (Levy 1979), the analysis proceeds from categories of professional values to the application of ethical theory.

WITHHOLDING INFORMATION FROM THOSE PLANNING TO INTERMARRY

As it considers how to operationalize the "J" in Jewish family services, a Jewish family service (JFS) agency had to confront the implications of intermarriage for its mission, policies, and ongoing service to clients. The agency's stated mission is "to strengthen Jewish individual and family life and promote Jewish identity." The following JFS policy statement (Jewish Family Service 1991) illustrates the interface between the agency's Jewish dimension and professional social work concerns, and the potential for conflict between them:

> When Jewishly sensitive life-cycle or potentially controversial issues arise in a residential service, counseling session, or other JFS-sponsored setting, the professional staff at JFS should be sufficiently trained and expected to:
> • identify and present the Jewish dimension and/or conflict in values which the particular dilemma raises (e.g. life-cycle issues of personal status, such as a prospective mixed marriage, divorce, unwanted pregnancy, etc.);
> • if appropriate, refer the client to a rabbi of his/her choice or to one made available through a JFS roster of rabbinic leaders, according to the individual's preferred branch of Judaism;
> • respect the social work process and the client's ultimate decision concerning this dilemma, regardless of what that final decision is;
> • (exceptions may be made when this is judged to be clinically contraindicated)

A staff seminar on ethics discussed the case of a prospective mixed marriage. Two policies were stated at the outset. Both the Project on Intermarriage (co-sponsored with the Board of Rabbis) and the Jewish Information Service, a community information office of JFS, are prohibited by agreement with the Board of Rabbis from furnishing information about rabbis and cantors in the community who are known to officiate at mixed marriages. Individual social workers, however, may use their own discretion in disseminating such information to a prospective couple. There is as yet no agency policy permitting or restricting such information in the counseling situation; the decision lies with the social workers themselves. The following question focused the value and ethical analysis: Is it ethical for the social worker to withhold this information from a couple contemplating intermarriage when the couple asks for it?

Categories of Professional Values

In chapter 1, professional values were classified into three groups (Levy 1973): preferred conceptions of people, preferred outcomes for people, and preferred instrumentalities for dealing with people.

Though there are other parties to the issue, the social worker, the agency, and the rabbinic community were selected because the conflict is highlighted among them (see table 7). Since the couple constituted the client, they were not included because this classification focuses on values concerning the client. The client is the object of the social worker's and agency's values. It is their preferred conceptions, outcomes, and instrumentalities regarding the client with which we are concerned.

However, it is important to point out the client's perspective. The couple's needs and the consumer-driven orientation currently prevalent in social services obligate the agency to respond. Clearly, prospective mixed-married couples who ask for the names of marriage officiators do so with the expectation that the agency will provide such a list. By requesting these names, the couple expresses a desire to gain Jewish communal sanction of their marriage and perhaps also to affiliate with the community and to raise their children as Jews. The request for a wedding under Jewish auspices may also be in response to the insistence of parents and grandparents. Whatever their motivation (and their motives should be explored in the counseling situation), the couple's request for the list ethically obligates the agency to provide it.

The Social Worker

Social workers prefer to view this couple as having dignity, and as capable of making competent decisions concerning their marriage.

From the social workers' perspective, the preferred outcome for the couple is their personal happiness. Some staff members would like the couple to lead a Jewish life, whereas others are prepared to leave the decision up to them. For some social workers, personal values and agency values coalesce in their desire to see the couple join the Jewish community. Other social workers are able to separate their personal values from their professional values in freeing the couple to decide the way they themselves want to go.

Table 7: Values Classification of Intermarriage Policy by Social Worker, Agency, and Rabbinic Community

	Preferred Conceptions of people	Preferred Outcomes for People	Preferred Instrumentalities for Working with People
Social Worker	Dignity Capable of making decisions, responsible for those decisions, capable of leading own way of life	Happiness Lead a Jewish life Lead a life according to their own wishes	Non-judgmental Self-determination Provide information
Agency	Dignity Capable of making decisions, responsible for those decisions, capable of leading own way of life, Jewish partner capable of creating Jewish family life	Become a Jewish family, affiliate with Jewish community, identify as Jews, prevent intermarriage	Non-judgmental Self-determination Not provide information
Rabbinic Community	Dignity, right to make own decisions, violating biblical norms, eroding fabric of Jewish life	Prevention of intermarriage, in conflict over conversion of non-Jewish partner and family membership in synagogues	Not provide information

Social workers' preferred instrumentalities are to be nonjudgmental, to support self-determination, and to serve as a resource.

They ought to have no professional preference regarding the choice of a mate. Their role is to help clients make a decision that is best for them and to provide information toward that end. Consequently, social workers value giving the information that the couple seeks. Some staff resisted the instrumental value of providing information because they believed that it would encourage intermarriage. This reflected the preference of personal values over professional values, but it may also have derived from their strong identification with the Jewish purposes of the agency.

The Agency

As a social work agency, JFS supports all the preferred conceptions of the social workers on its staff. The couple is seen as responsible and capable of making decisions that will affect their future married life. The agency also views itself as an instrument of the Jewish community that is committed to Jewish continuity. Due to this commitment, the agency's preferred conception of the religiously mixed couple is that they are capable of leading a Jewish way of life and raising a Jewish family. The agency also wants to view them as potentially belonging to, and identifying with, the Jewish community. Among its preferred outcomes is the prevention of intermarriage, but where it cannot prevent a mixed marriage from occurring, it encourages the couple to affiliate with the Jewish community.

The agency's conflict between its professional social work identity and its Jewish communal identity also surfaces in its preferred instrumentalities. In providing a professional service to clients, the agency maintains a nonjudgmental approach and seeks to foster client self-determination. However, through its Jewish Information Service, the agency denies requests to provide information about marriage officiators to couples because it cannot condone an action that may be construed as supporting intermarriage.

Although the agency has not instituted this policy in the counseling situation, but leaves it to the discretion of the social workers, the social workers know the preferences of the agency. Theoretically, the social workers are granted the freedom to act according to professional judgment and client need, but practically, the ethos of Jewish communal life that pervades the agency, in effect, delimits that freedom.

Rabbinic Community

The local rabbinic community consists of rabbis who represent a wide spectrum of religious ideologies. However, though they are diverse in their belief systems and religious practices, they agree that intermarriage is forbidden by Jewish law and is a threat to Jewish continuity. A prime function of Jewish communal institutions, including federations, synagogues, Jewish community centers, Jewish family services, and Jewish educational institutions is to discourage and prevent intermarriage.

In their preferred conceptions of the prospective mixed-married couple, the rabbis value the couple's dignity and right to make decisions that will affect their life together. Although the couple's self-determination is respected, the rabbis conceive of their decision to intermarry as a negative value. They view them as violating a biblical norm and eroding the fabric of Jewish life.

The rabbis' preferred outcome for the counseling situation is the dissolution of the relationship, resulting in the prevention of intermarriage. If that is unsuccessful, a second preferred outcome is the conversion of the non-Jewish spouse. This is becoming more difficult to effect because mixed-married couples are gaining wider acceptance into synagogues sans conversion.

To achieve these outcomes, the rabbis prefer that the social worker not provide the information. With this action, the social worker conveys the agency's and the community's negative valuation of intermarriage. The rabbis hope that this action will deter the couple from proceeding with the marriage.

The rabbis view the agency, the federation, and the synagogue as part of the Jewish institutional network. All need to work together to prevent the erosion of Jewish life through intermarriage. Though intermarriage rates are rising, the rabbis still hope that it could be thwarted by what professionals do and say while counseling prospective mixed-married couples. The rabbinic community would interpret the pro-referral stance of JFS as support for intermarriage, which cannot be countenanced by the organized Jewish community.

A Question of Ethics

The values of the social worker, the agency, and the rabbinic community coalesce to focus the ethical question: may the information be withheld from clients? In chapter 2, deontological and utilitarian theories were utilized in the decision-making process in support of ethical principles. Deontological theory posits the inherent rightness of an action, for reasons other than their consequences, based on such moral principles or prima facie duties as fidelity, nonmaleficence, beneficence, and justice. Utilitarians maintain that the moral rightness of an action is determined by its consequences (Beauchamp and Childress 1994).

In this case, deontological social workers would provide the information. This is based on the principle of beneficence—that we have a duty to contribute to the welfare of others. The client is asking for information about a community resource, and the social worker's function is to provide that resource. That is the ethical thing to do.

The application of deontological theory may also lead to the opposite conclusion. The social worker's employment in a Jewish agency that is deeply committed to Jewish continuity may serve as a rationale for not providing information. A Jewish agency should not promote intermarriage by divulging the names of officiators. This is based on the principle of nonmaleficence—not causing harm to the continuity of Jewish communal life. This principle, which is directed toward the Jewish community, is weaker than the principle of beneficence which is directed toward the client.

Providing information to a couple contemplating intermarriage does not inevitably lead to intermarriage, nor does withholding the information prevent it. They could obtain the information elsewhere. It is, therefore, not self-evident deontologically that the social worker in a Jewish agency should withhold the information because it promotes intermarriage.

According to Ross (1930), while we intuit moral principles, we do not intuit what is right in the situation; rather, we have to find the greatest balance of right over wrong. In this situation, the greatest balance seems to favor the principle of beneficence (i.e., service) over nonmaleficence (i.e., not causing harm) because it meets the clients' need to know and contributes to their welfare.

Social work utilitarians need to investigate the consequences for the various parties. By withholding the information when couples ask for it, the social worker may alienate them from the agency and the Jewish community. Couples say they want a rabbi to marry them in order to be part of the Jewish community. From a utilitarian perspective, giving the names could lead to the greater good and is the ethical thing to do.

The consequences for the agency may be more harmful. Sensitive to its image in the Jewish community, the agency could be condemned by more Jewishly identified factions who may threaten to reduce their financial support. If their requests are spurned, couples may be alienated from Jewish communal life. Other prospective interfaith couples may not seek services from the agency.

It is also conceivable that positive consequences could ensue. The couple may break up, and the agency can claim a victory against intermarriage, thus solidifying its image among the more traditional groups in the Jewish community.

Conclusion

Although the decision to provide information on intermarriage officiators to interfaith couples may appear academic, as they could obtain it on their own, studying the values and ethics underlying the decision is a useful exercise. The decision is complicated by the fact that the social worker is employed by a Jewishly committed agency, influenced by a rabbinic community, that sees its mission as promoting Jewish values and strengthening Jewish family life. The prospect of intermarriage creates ideological conflict between the values and ethics of social work and the values and ethics of Judaism. When an agency subscribes to both, it is caught in a bind.

The social worker, too, is caught in a bind. The social worker in this agency subscribes to the values of the profession and the Jewish community, which do not completely coincide in this case. Therefore, when the agency places the onus of the decision to disclose the information upon the social worker, he or she must wrestle with the conflicting values and ethics in the dilemma. The decision should not be based on personal values, but on prioritizing professional values. Basing action on professional values is the hallmark of the professional.

SERVING INTERMARRIED COUPLES AND
THEIR FAMILIES

An executive of a Jewish family service anguished over the intermarriage policy contemplated by his agency.

A good example of an ethical dilemma is the phenomenon of
intermarriage. In terms of Jewish values, intermarriage
evokes strong feelings and is not to be encouraged. Nonethe-
less, there is a striking presence of families who have intermarried and others who are vulnerable to future
intermarriage.

A lot of anguish is being experienced by families with an
intermarried member, due to the stance of the Jewish community. This ranges from the extreme of broad acceptance
and liberal understanding to the other extreme, where people talk about sitting *shiva* (mourning) and having no association with the intermarried. Somewhere in the middle are the
innocent victims—the parents, the grandparents, children
born to the intermarriage, and even the couple, who find
themselves in a relationship that has far-reaching repercus-
sions in the Jewish community.

In the synagogue, when there is an intermarriage, do you
wish the couple *mazel tov?* Do you wish the couple's parents
mazel tov? When a child is born, do you set up a two-track system whereby you welcome the child of the Jewish mother
into the ranks, but not of the non-Jewish mother?

What is the role of the family agency in responding to the
pain of the couple and the extended family? What is our role
with the synagogues and Jewish schools who look to us for
guidance in this issue? What should be the response of the
Jewish family agency as we move into the community and do
Jewish family-life education and therapy? In our response to
the people who bring this issue to us, are we in some measure
supporting and accepting the very concept of intermarriage
when we attempt to provide relief?

How aggressive should we be in moving into the community to develop services to this sizable and growing population?

Q: Why should it be a dilemma to serve the parents and the grandparents?

A: Do you help them to better accept the intermarriage? What message are you transmitting as a representative of the Jewish communal structure in terms of values? On the other hand, as a caseworker, you believe in self-determination and in being nonjudgmental. The seemingly neutral course would be to help the people to identify what they're struggling with.

As a Jewish agency, we do take a stand. We do not want to do anything that will encourage intermarriage, but by the same token we have a firm conviction that people who are experiencing conflict and distress deserve to be responded to in a way that will offer them some relief. However, in offering them the relief, do we in fact encourage the perpetuation of intermarriage?

*Resolution.*We have taken a deep breath, moved into the community, and sponsored workshops and groups. We have conducted groups with rabbis who are facing this problem in their congregations, parents of children who have intermarried, and grandparents who are raising a child from the intermarriage who may not be halakhically Jewish because the parents have split and are not available to raise the child. A non-Jewish child being raised by a Jewish grandparent is brought to a religious school. We have not offered groups to the intermarried or about-to-be-married couples, but we are exploring this. However, in our counseling services, we very often see intermarried couples.

Discussion

Intermarriage is of concern to parents and families, professionals and lay leaders in federations, synagogues, Jewish schools, Jewish community centers, and Jewish family agencies who care about the erosion of Jewish life and struggle to stem its tide (Mayer and Sheingold 1979; Huberman 1985).

This dilemma, presented with a troubled conscience by the administrator of a family agency, confronts many family agencies. It is larger than the question of whether to counsel intermarried couples, for it touches upon agency image and interagency collaboration. It encompasses ethical and practice considerations.

Ethical Issues

The ethical dilemma raises the question of whether or not to serve the intermarried. The issues in this case parallel the issues in the previous case of giving information about marriage officiators to interfaith couples. In ethical terms, is it right not to serve this population? This dilemma is based upon conflicting values which are esteemed by the agency. As a social work–based agency, it subscribes to the profession's Code of Ethics, which prohibits social workers from discriminating against clients due to religion and marital status (National Association of Social Workers 1980). The professional esteems the individual's right to self-determination, which includes the choice of marriage partner. Self-determination is a value that stems from a preferred conception of human beings as capable of actualizing themselves. Based upon these professional values to which the agency and its professional staff subscribe, along with the ethical principle of beneficence, it is wrong for the agency to refuse to serve the intermarried and their families. This stance is supported by deontological theory that common sense and a commitment to the social worker–client relationship forbids a social welfare agency from discriminating against potential clients.

The conflicting value stems from the agency's role as an instrument for furthering the goals of the Jewish community. The community's most prominent goal is to continue as a viable entity. Intermarriage is perceived as a threat to its continuity. As an instrument of the community, the agency values positive Jewish commitment and strong Jewish identity. Continuity is preferred to extinction, and the preservation of the Jewish family is preferred to its dissolution. Serving the intermarried may have a negative effect on Jewish communal life, for it may perpetuate marriages that do not statistically contribute to the enhancement of Jewish life and the socialization of children to Jewishness (Crohn, n.d.). Ethically speaking, the agency is permitted to refuse services to this group based on the utilitarian principles of preventing harm and fidelity to its mission as an instrument of Jewish continuity.

Practice Issues

In addition to the ethical issues in this case, there are practice considerations. If an intermarried couple come for counseling, if their parents seek help with their feelings and conflicts, if Jewish grandparents are ambivalent about caring for their non-Jewish grandchildren, the professional staff of the Jewish family agency are required to deal with these problems. They are expected to explore the Jewish issue as a central dynamic in their coming to the Jewish agency.

Interagency relationships are related to the practice issues. The administrator needs to formulate the agency's policy on intermarriage, so that it could be communicated to participants in Jewish family-life education forums in Jewish schools and synagogues. The policy will most certainly affect the agency's public image, which may determine its effectiveness in serving the Jewish community.

One way of approaching this practice dilemma is to discuss it with the executives of other Jewish institutions. Synagogues have intermarried families, and parents and grandparents of intermarried; Jewish schools have children of intermarried couples among their student body. In fact, there is hardly a Jewish organization or family which does not have gentiles in its midst. Family agencies should not bear the brunt of the problem alone, but should seek out other agencies to map common policy.

In the resolution of the ethical dilemma—whether serving the intermarried is right or wrong—the agency's actual stance falls somewhere between the two alternatives. The complexities of human needs and the desire of many Jews to remain Jews while assimilating to the larger culture require avoiding taking extreme positions on most social problems affecting the Jewish community. This is due to the pluralistic nature of Jewish life and the non-halakhic auspices of the family agency. The agency is not a religious institution. It serves a wide spectrum of Jews in the community and strives to be inclusive rather than exclusive. Its approach to community divisions is to search out the common ground in public discourse and to synthesize competing values and ethics.

The agency is leaning toward adopting a principle that will guide its position on this issue:

When a Jewish family agency is confronted with requests to serve the intermarried and their families, it should let it be known that, though it does not condone the practice, it offers programs and services to help them deal with their problems.

This principle might also be communicated to other Jewish institutions in the community.

CONCLUSION

Intermarriage is an issue that will not go away. It will persist to challenge lay and professional Jewish communal leaders to find ways to stem its tide and deal with its consequences. There are mixed reactions. While the majority of leaders perceive intermarriage to have negative effects on the Jewish future, some view the phenomenon as making it possible to bring mixed Jewish families into the mainstream of Jewish life through active outreach and education (Medding et al. 1992).

The increasing acceptance of the inevitability of intermarriage is having an impact on the services of family agencies, Jewish community centers, synagogues, and Jewish schools. The intermarried are being served in larger numbers without the attendant publicity. While some synagogues can justify their refusal to serve this group on religious grounds, it is ethically difficult for a secular Jewish agency that subscribes to social work values to refuse to serve them. Serving the intermarried does not free the agency from confronting value and ethical dilemmas due to its commitment to perpetuate Jewish life. These conflicts should continue to challenge lay leaders and professional staff in their deliberations about the agency's philosophy, mission, and services.

Chapter 15

Ethical Dilemmas in Jewish Education

In recent years, the trend in Jewish education has shifted from afternoon schools to day schools. Most day schools today are operated under Orthodox auspices, but Conservative and Reform day schools have also expanded. There appears to be wide recognition among all four religious movements and among Jewish communal leaders that intensive Jewish education is necessary for combatting assimilation and maintaining Jewish continuity.

Until recently, there has been little statistical evidence to support Jewish education's claims of success in ensuring Jewish continuity. A study in the 1970s found that there was a noticeable difference in Jewish life-style between groups that received a formal Jewish education and groups that did not (Ribner 1978). Grad (1978) contends that a data bank and criteria for evaluation are lacking, thus precluding an objective assessment of accomplishments. He urges a moratorium on curriculum development, and instead, investment of collective efforts in the development of criteria and tools for the evaluation of results.

As if in response to the call for a formal evaluation of the effectiveness of Jewish education, Schiff and Schneider (1994*b*) conducted a major research study of the effects of day school education on adult Jewish behavior. All told, 8,536 graduates of twenty-six Jewish day schools were sampled. They discovered that there is a statistically significant relationship between Jewish day school attendance, adult Jewish behavior and involvement, endogamous marital patterns, and negative attitudes toward intermarriage. Only 4.5 percent of Jewish day school graduates married non-Jews, compared with 52 percent as reported in the National Jewish Population Survey (Council of Jewish Federations

1991*b*).

The results of this survey may or may not lay to rest the debate in the organized Jewish community regarding the effectiveness of day school education. That debate, fueled by the results of the National Jewish Population Survey, is part of a larger soul-searching effort among Jewish communal leaders concerning the best ways to ensure Jewish continuity. In response, the Council of Jewish Federations (CJF) established a Commission on Jewish Identity and Continuity in 1992 to help reverse the trend of assimilation and intermarriage. A significant number of communities have undertaken a variety of projects to deal with the issues of identity and continuity. Jewish education, in its myriad forms, is seen as the indispensable vehicle for strengthening Jewish life.

The debate concerning the effectiveness of Jewish education may be fueled by its unclear goals. The goal of ensuring Jewish continuity is a negative one; it aims to prevent the attrition of the Jewish community through assimilation and intermarriage. By adopting this goal, the community asserts that "what binds us together is a perception of common danger rather than a commitment to shared values" (Wurzburger 1978, p. 26). The primary goals of Jewish education should be the enhancement of "the quality of life of our children by endowing their existence with transcendent meaning and purpose" (ibid.).

In addition to the need for clarity in goals, Jewish education is concerned with the need for increased funding, particularly in difficult economic times (Feuerman 1983). In recent years, federations across North America have begun to allocate more resources to Jewish education (Spotts 1979; Schiff 1986). Resources have also been allocated to establish the Commission on Maximizing Jewish Educational Effectiveness of Jewish Community Centers, and to determine ways of educating adults and improving the quality and professionalism of Jewish education. To these ends, the Wexner Foundation, among others, has supported the recruitment and professional development of Jewish educators. There is wide recognition that the quality of Jewish education can only be enhanced by attracting qualified and committed teachers who will be paid decent wages and benefits.

Notwithstanding concerns for the economics and staffing of Jewish education, ideological and ethical issues exist. Some concern the diversity of values, beliefs, and practices among the religious denominations in the Jewish community. Other ethical issues, to be presented as case examples, concern accepting the children of intermarried couples in religious schools, marketing Jewish schools, teaching religious content in opposition to the ideology of the school, providing scholarships for those who do not need them, and the relationship between the central board of Jewish education and federation.

CHILD OF MIXED MARRIAGE IN A JEWISH SCHOOL

The administrator of a central board of Jewish education presents a difficult dilemma.

One of the ethical dilemmas that confronts us is the case of a child from a non-Jewish mother and a Jewish father who is sent to day or afternoon school for a Jewish education. Sometimes we only discover after the child is enrolled that the parents are intermarried and the mother is not Jewish. The problem is compounded because of the split in the Jewish community between those who maintain that only matrilineal descent confers Jewish identity, and those who believe that patrilineal descent does so too. Some recognize these children as Jews, and others do not. These situations occur frequently, because when these children are enrolled in the school, no one bothers to check into their background. The question arises as to whether the principal should ask the child to leave.

Some principals might try to persuade the parents to have the child converted. Some might object to this on principle. Conversion may be the ideal solution, but it is not so simple. The family may not be ready, and it would depend on the philosophy of the school and the religious identity of the lay leaders. I believe this dilemma will become more prominent as the years go on because of the diversity in the Jewish community.

Discussion
There are a number of interested parties in this case. The parents,

despite their different religious backgrounds, have decided that their child should receive a Jewish education. In the discussion that must have preceded this decision, the mother may have acceded to the father's insistence that their child be educated Jewishly, or she herself may have preferred to raise their child in her husband's religion. Sometimes Jewish education is irrelevant to the husband, and it only materializes through the non-Jewish wife's initiative. In choosing the Jewish school, the couple may not have been aware of the ideological conflict in the Jewish community over Jewish identity. Or perhaps they were assured by their Reform rabbi that the child would be considered Jewish if raised as a Jew. Whatever the background scenario, enrolling their child in a Jewish school expresses the family's value of their child having a Jewish identity and a sense of belonging to the Jewish community.

The decision by mixed-married parents to provide a Jewish education for their child is not a widespread practice. It is more common where one parent is a born Jew and the other a convert. Children of conversionary marriages are more likely to receive an intensive Jewish education, celebrate bar or bat mitzvah, and observe Jewish holidays than children who had one Jewish and one Gentile parent (Mayer and Sheingold 1983). Since the parents in the case example have defied the statistical trend, should they be encouraged to keep their child in the Jewish school to foster Jewish knowledge and identity, or should they be told to remove the child because, according to some groups, the child is not Jewish?

The Jewish community is split between the Orthodox and Conservative on one side, and the Reform and Reconstructionist on the other regarding the legitimacy of conferring Jewish identity through patrilineal descent. Orthodox and Conservative Jews uphold the tradition of matrilineal descent; this child is, therefore, halakhically not Jewish. From their perspective, it is halakhically and morally wrong for a non-Jewish child to attend a Jewish school (Schwartzbaum 1988, pp. 155–163). This policy is consistent with deontological theory, which supports actions as inherently right or wrong, without regard for consequences (Beauchamp and Childress 1989). The halakhic stance is basically deontological: accepting the child in the school is wrong.

Keeping this child in a Jewish school may have negative consequences, as it creates a false sense of Jewish identity. The child grows up with an identity as a Jew, when, in fact, major groups in the Jewish community deny that identity. According to utilitarian theory, if enrollment in the school may lead to greater harm—deception, rejection, and a confused identity—than benefit for the child, the action is deemed to be unethical.

Reform and Reconstructionist Jews contend that there has been a Jewish tradition of patrilineal descent; the community needs to accept as Jews children of mixed parentage in order to be inclusive rather than exclusive (Schindler 1986). The child, therefore, is considered Jewish.

Once defined as Jewish, the child is entitled to a Jewish education. Enrollment in the school is ethically consistent with deontological theory because it is the right policy for a Jewish child, and with utilitarian theory because it will lead to good consequences—a positive Jewish identity.

The issue of patrilineal descent is one of the most divisive in the Jewish community. It portends a time in the near future when the children of the unions of non-Jewish mothers and Jewish fathers will not be able to marry Jews whose mothers are Jewish. The polarization of religious camps is bringing in its wake an unabashed delegitimization of ideological denominations other than one's own (Chanover 1986). Concerted efforts are being made to bring the denominations together to promote mutual respect and understanding (National Jewish Center for Learning and Leadership 1986), but these efforts did not prevent the Synagogue Council of America from disbanding due to ideological differences among the denominations.

The Jewish school serves as an instrument of the Jewish community. Its ideological complexion is determined by the composition of the board of directors, who represent the community. If it is a community school, with the board representing all factions of the Jewish community, it would need to contend with the ideological and political controversy over patrilineal descent. The decision regarding the child's continuance in the school is ideally the board's. If the board and the administration are ideologically affiliated with a particular denomination, they will be influenced by the policies of that denomination.

The principal's conflict may be of a different order. The principal may be personally Orthodox or Conservative and therefore espouses belief in matrilineal descent. The day school may be a community school that reflects the spectrum of Jewish communal life where the board is not ideologically committed to the tenets of traditional Judaism. The principal's conflict may exist on two levels: between personal and professional values, and between the principal and the board. Personal values commit the principal to an action that calls for the ouster of the child from the school; professional values commit the principal to educate the child of a mixed Jewish family that desires to affiliate with the Jewish community.

The principal's personal values may be in conflict with the values of the board which calls for the child's retention in the school. The ethical dilemma arises from the competing values of the concerned parties.

The question that produces the ethical dilemma concerns the right action. Is it right to exclude the child from acquiring a Jewish education? Because of the conflicting values maintained by the different parties—parents, child, board, Jewish community, principal—the ethical decision is not clear. What is right for one party may be wrong for the other. The right ethical action in this case may be ultimately determined by the ideology of the school board.

Resolution

Converting the child to Judaism would relieve the tension among the parties, but it is not known whether the parents would agree. If they refuse, the action should be based on the ethics of the situation.

The respondent offered no resolution to the ethical dilemma because there is no clear ethical principle. In social work ethics, the client is the primary concern of the social worker. In Jewish education, the child is the primary client. It is the child's needs that would inform the ethical stance of the educator. The child's religious identity determines the right to a Jewish education. The agonizing question is: what is the child's religious identity?

Neither deontological theory nor utilitarian theory assists in the ethical decision. This is due to the intractability of the value conflict. Perhaps, as Lewis (1984) contends, more knowledge is needed. The more that is known about the values and needs of the concerned parties, the more equipped they will be to render an ethical decision.

"SELLING" THE JEWISH SCHOOL

At this time the day school is the most intensive form of Jewish education. As an administrator in a bureau of Jewish education, I try to sell the day school to the community as the best form of Jewish education. The dilemma for me is that sometimes we do a little overselling, and we are not sure that the day school does what it is supposed to do —make an impact on the child's feelings about himself as a Jew, and developing a commitment to the Jewish people. Maybe we're selling the Jewish community a false bill of goods.

We have a commitment to tell the absolute truth. It is not that we are lying, it is just that we are not sure that the truth we are selling is real. This bothers me because I strongly believe that the only hope we have for survival is through Jewish education.

Discussion

The issue in this case is truth-telling. It recalls the truth-in-packaging laws that protect consumers from manufacturers who overstate the case for their products. Jewish education is viewed as a product that requires marketing. Since this interview took place before the Schiff and Schneider study (1994*ab*), the administrator possessed little hard data that substantiated day schools' claims of success in imbuing Jewish identity and commitment. He suspected that the message being communicated was totally truthful. This educator's dilemma is whether it is ethical to make claims for a "product" whose benefits have not been substantiated.

Though educators cannot prove that day school education does what it claims to do, their experiential wisdom and professional judgments inform them that children who attend day schools, as opposed to afternoon and Sunday schools, seem to be more knowledgeable about Judaism, feel more Jewish, and participate in more Jewish activities (Grad 1978).

To determine whether there is an ethical dilemma when

assumptions are conveyed as truths to an unsuspecting public, we need to delineate the underlying values. One value is truth-telling. Since values lead to a commitment to action (Levy 1973), in publicizing the day school, the educator should not make grandiose claims for its achievements. Instead, the message should convey the assumptions and assessments without asserting them as true facts.

Another value is all-day *Jewish* education as opposed to public *secular* education. The school's commitment to this value expresses itself in advertising the benefits of a Jewish day school education in contrast to a public school education. The differences need not be empirically confirmed, because the contrasts between the educational programs are obvious.

Resolution
Resolution of the ethical dilemma could be supported by both deontological and utilitarian theory. Intuitively, we should tell the truth because it is the right thing to do, and it needs no other justification. This obligation stems from the prima facie duty of fidelity (Binkly 1961) to the people served. Falsification in advertising is immoral. On the other hand, is it considered a lie when claims are made about a product that have not yet been substantiated by scientific evidence? It would seem that the impressionistic evidence in this situation is not in the category of falsehood.

In the utilitarian view, the ethical act is that which brings about the greater good. In this case, claims that rely on practice experiences and professional judgments not empirically substantiated may be permitted if they might motivate parents to send their children to the day school. The greater good is attained when, as a result of their Jewish education, children grow up to lead Jewish lives and raise their children as Jews.

In the resolution of this dilemma, the educator can adopt the deontological or utilitarian approach to support his inclination to "sell" the day school to the Jewish community, though he does not possess statistical data to confirm his professional judgments.

TEACHING CONFLICTING RELIGIOUS CONTENT
It is a commonplace that religious pluralism permeates Jewish

communal life. Each religious denomination maintains an ideology concerning belief and practice that it desires to inculcate into its adherents. In its religious school system, the denomination will ideally hire teachers who conform to its ideology in their private lives so as to avoid dissonance in the classroom.

The ideal is not always achieved. Because of a teacher shortage, schools have been forced to hire teachers whose ideology differs from their own. This can create a value conflict and an ethical dilemma for the teachers.

> A teacher who describes herself ideologically as "centrist Orthodox" is teaching in a Reform congregation. The subject of kashrut arises in the classroom. As one who observes the laws of kashrut, the teacher feels a personal and religious obligation to expose the children to the philosophy and the laws behind that mitzvah. Yet, the philosophy of the institution does not embrace kashrut as mandatory. Is it ethical for the teacher to teach and encourage the students to practice the laws of kashrut when this violates the position of the Reform movement and the local congregation?

Discussion

The teacher's dilemma is located in the conflict between her personal and professional values, discussed in chapter 6, and within her professional values. The severity of the conflict is determined by the depth of her personal convictions and her commitment to professional values.

On the personal level, she may be among those modern Orthodox Jews who do not aspire to impose their values on other Jews, even in a teaching role. The conflict is, therefore, minimized because the teacher could point out that the Torah commands laws pertaining to permissible and forbidden foods, but not all Jews subscribe to them. This approach takes into account the pluralistic nature of Jewish life and the prevalence of choice in observance. It also conforms to the professional value of adhering to agency policy in the service of the student.

The teacher might be among those modern Orthodox Jews who would exhort students to follow the mitzvot in the Torah, regardless of the school's auspices, because they feel deeply about the value of performing mitzvot and bringing Jews closer to the Torah and to God. The teacher in this group would have serious conflict between her personal convictions and her professional commitment to abide by the policy of the school.

The strength of the teacher's professional identity is another factor in the analysis of the conflict. Most teachers in congregational and day schools are not licensed, nor do they possess professional credentials in teaching. A weak professional identity may desensitize them to the seriousness of violating school policy and the teachers' code of ethics. They may not be aware that they are acting unethically.

A licensed teacher, with graduate school credentials, might experience greater incongruence between personal and professional values. A commitment to professional values is a given; when it clashes with deeply imbued personal values, it is difficult to predict the outcome. However, a competent professional teacher will not permit her personal values to override her professional function. She will find a way to reconcile the two value systems by prioritizing her professional function and leaving her personal values at home.

The teacher might also seek a compromise. Instead of teaching her students how to practice the laws of kashrut, she can merely convey the philosophy, laws, and customs that regulate this mode of living, and the different practices among Jews. The teacher may express her personal commitment to kashrut observance and advise the students that it is only her personal stance and may not be applicable to their and their parents' life-style.

Resolution

The resolution of the dilemma inclines toward the prohibition of teaching a doctrine against the religious ideology of the school. It is the school's responsibility to inform prospective teachers of this policy at the hiring interview. Ethical norms require teachers not to violate the policy of the school by teaching an opposing doctrine.

This ethical obligation obtains in other situations of ideological conflict, e.g., a Conservative teacher in an Orthodox school, a Reform teacher in a Conservative school, or any variation thereof. A teacher who cannot abide by the ideology of the hiring institution has the option of not taking the job, and should not attempt to subvert the institution's ideology.

SCHOLARSHIPS FOR THE NON-NEEDY

The high cost of Jewish education (Monson and Feldman 1991–92) has exacerbated economic pressures on young families who struggle to send their children to day schools while public school education is free. Ideologically, many young couples share a commitment to Jewish education, but they may not act on it due to financial constraints.

Tuition scholarships are offered to encourage parents to send their children to Jewish schools. These are based on financial need, which parents usually demonstrate by producing a tax return. Not all parents act ethically in requesting scholarship funds.

> Mr. Cohen drives a Lincoln Continental. Yet he claims that he cannot afford to pay the full tuition for his child and produces his W-4, which supports his claim. His car is business-related; he asserts that he has no money and requests a scholarship.
>
> The choice for the school is whether or not to give Mr. Cohen's child a scholarship. If the school turns down the scholarship request, the child will likely be enrolled in a public school. If it does offer a scholarship and the word gets out, the community will become very upset and accuse the school of impropriety in the use of communal funds.

Discussion

A number of details are missing from this scenario. What does Mr. Cohen's tax return look like? Does it show him earning a ridiculously low salary for the life-style that his family leads? If so, this would seem to indicate that his is a cash business, and he earned more than what is reported. If the scholarship committee is dubious about his earnings and refuses the request, it would be consistent with its policy that only those deserving of the scholarship should receive it. If he threatens to send his child to public school, the committee need feel no guilt over its actions. If Mr. Cohen really wanted his child to obtain a Jewish education, he would find a way to finance it.

The committee might be guided by deontological theory and do what it deems to be right in the situation. It is right to reject a scholarship request from someone who is deemed capable of paying the tuition. It is right to reserve communal funds for those who are unable to pay. Utilitarian thinking could produce the same result. The greater good is served when scarce scholarship funds are reserved for the truly needy.

If, however, Mr. Cohen produces a tax return that reflects a reasonable income, and he claims that he cannot afford the tuition, the committee might give him the benefit of the doubt and grant his request. The luxury car might be attributed to a lease, a gift from a relative, or another source. The committee might also be guided by both ethical theories because they arrive at the same conclusion. It is right to support a parent who is financially strapped, and the positive consequences of granting the scholarship will result in providing the child with a Jewish education.

CENTRAL BOARD OF JEWISH EDUCATION–FEDERATION RELATIONSHIP

With lay and professional leaders paying increasing attention to promoting Jewish continuity, central boards of Jewish education have taken the spotlight in the federation network. Jewish communal leadership, running scared concerning the viability of the coming generations, has called for creative programs that will promote Jewish identification and strengthen Jewish identity. Jewish education is looked to as the vehicle for achieving these ends. As a result, relationships between central boards of Jewish education and federations have become more solidified, but they are not without their political and ethical strains.

1. Federation's policy is that it should primarily provide services to the populations that tend to support it in its fundraising campaigns. Consequently, the Orthodox community, which tends not to support federations as much as the other denominations, should receive fewer services.

The dilemma for the central board of Jewish education is

that it is a beneficiary of federation's largesse and responsible for following its policies. But the board, as an autonomous agency within the federation, claims the right to determine its own policies regarding the recipients of services. The board wants all its constituents, including the Orthodox, to receive services, which should not be contingent upon the size of contributions.

2. The emphasis at federation of late is on strengthening informal Jewish education, such as Jewish community centers, over formal education in the classrooms.

The board would like to strengthen formal Jewish education because it believes that the bulk of learning takes place in the classroom.

Discussion

1. The conflict between the central board and federation conforms to an ethical dilemma because it is based on conflicting values. Federation wants to reward its supporters with increased services and decrease services to nonsupporters. Since resources are limited, allocation decisions may be based on the degree of philanthropic support.

The central board argues that federation, as the umbrella organization of the Jewish community, is responsible for serving all groups, regardless of their degree of support. It is not as if the Orthodox do not contribute at all; they do not contribute according to their potential and numbers. The board is, therefore, confronted with the dilemma of allocating federation's grant to the Orthodox schools according to its own criteria.

The board resolves the dilemma by asserting its autonomy as an independent agency within the federation network. It claims jurisdiction over allocating resources to the areas of direst need, including Orthodox schools. In this dilemma, the ethical principle of autonomy overrides the ethical principle of benevolence, which is closely allied with federation's paternalism. The board's autonomy is an expression of independence and the right to make decisions based on its greater expertise in educational administration.

2. Another value conflict revolves around the preference for informal vs. formal Jewish education. Federations have been

investing resources and talent to enhance informal Jewish education because they reach many more people, including adults and
families, who may not be Jewishly identified, and who are not
reached by formal education.

The central board of Jewish education is the umbrella organization of Jewish schools where instruction is carried out primarily by
formal educational methods. Its target for allocating staff and
resources is the classroom, which is the most effective location for
inculcating Jewish values and traditions.

On the surface, this appears not to be a conflict. The board is
not asked to disburse its funds to Jewish community centers
(JCCs) and other informal Jewish educational settings. Federation
has the jurisdiction to allocate funds to JCCs to enhance their
informal Jewish programming. The board can continue to spend
its funds on the schools under its jurisdiction. However, a
dilemma arises when the board, having reduced its staff due to
budget cutbacks, is asked by JCCs and other institutions to assign
staff to help them carry out informal Jewish education in their
agencies. Should the board assign its depleted staff to the informal
system or stick with its major constituents—the formal system?

This conflict between federation and the board appears to be in
the practice arena rather than the ethical realm. It is a conflict
over what is the best way to deploy staff of the central board.

The conflict can be resolved by federation's infusion of additional funding so that more staff either at the board or at the JCCs
can serve as resources for informal educational programming. A
compromise solution, sans additional funding, is for the board to
allocate some time from the staff's regular assignment to the JCCs
and other agencies. The latter solution benefits neither the formal
nor the informal system because both are shortchanged.

Rather than maintain an impasse, both agencies need to look
for ways to work together during difficult economic times. There
is a healthy respect for the work of Jewish educators. "The Federations will continue all that is possible to support you in this criti-
cally important enterprise: the insuring of Jewish continuity"
(Solender 1983).

CONCLUSION

During these times of reduced fund-raising and budget cutbacks, the demands for productivity in the Jewish educational enterprise are increasing. The cry has become louder of late because the organized Jewish community is fearful for its discontinuity due to rampant assimilation and intermarriage. There appears to be near unanimous agreement that the key to Jewish survival is intensive Jewish education in its myriad forms.

While new services and studies abound, and the frantic pace of developing programs to strengthen Jewish identity goes into high gear, issues arise on a daily basis in the classroom and in the administration of the Jewish educational system that evoke ethical and moral dilemmas for practitioners. The cases presented represent but a small sample of some of these dilemmas.

Whether the dilemma in the classroom concerns the administrator's agonizing over expelling a child born of a non-Jewish mother, marketing the day school as the most effective form of Jewish education when all the data are not yet in, conflicts between a teacher's personal values and those of the school administration, giving scholarships to parents who are suspected of not being needy, or resolving fundamental differences in the central board's relationship with federation—guidelines are available that could assist in their resolution.

When the conflict emerges, the underlying values of the conflicting parties need to be analyzed. These provide the base for the ethical dilemma, which is a choice between two actions based on conflicting values. Ethical theories and principles are then applied to illuminate the arguments. The decision is up to the parties involved, after having proceeded through an organized, scholarly deliberation in decision-making.

Chapter 16

Prospects and Problems

This book has been an attempt to encompass a wide range of ethical dilemmas as they emerge in the daily routines of Jewish communal service agencies. The list is neither exhaustive nor comprehensive. Nor can it be, as new dilemmas emerge daily. It is believed that the range of cases presented evokes the basic conceptual and practical dimensions of ethical decision-making.

The following topics highlight the ethical issues in the cases presented:

1. The lay person's exercise of power to circumvent rules and regulations is manifest in circumventing the waiting list and in fund-raising.
2. Federation's relationship to its constituent agencies is highlighted in the distribution of funds to agencies in a changing community, and in conjunction with the central board of Jewish education.
3. Value and ethical dilemmas in the relationship between the professional and the client are seen in the role of values in determining agency policy, placing an elderly couple in a nursing home, and acting paternalistically with elderly clients.
4. Conflicts between the professional and the agency are analyzed in the Jewish educational setting, where a teacher taught subjects that opposed the school's ideology, and in chapters 4 and 5.
5. The impact of pluralism on services to the Jewish community is noted in the Jewish school's deliberation over accepting children of mixed-married parents, and an

agency's right to withhold information from a prospective interfaith couple.

6. Personal-professional conflicts surface over professionals' time commitments to family and to work, and in the difficulty they have in reconciling their personal friendships with their professional duties.

7. Talmudic and ethical principles are applied to the allocation of scarce resources, a perennial and dogged problem, for the resettlement of Jews from the former Soviet Union.

8. There are ethical issues that arise in serving certain groups of people because of moral considerations in Jewish law. These include the mentally handicapped, homosexuals, and the intermarried.

9. Halakhah (Jewish law) occupies a place of prominence in deliberations on serving the intermarried, operating center activities on the Sabbath, and center kashrut policies. It operates subliminally in other issues due to the commitment of Jewish agencies to uphold Jewish values.

10. Jewish agencies, as sectarian agencies with nonsectarian membership policies, face difficult decisions regarding the acceptance of public funds for their operations. Though the practice is widespread, it still poses an ethical dilemma for federation's funding only Jewish activities or leveraging to acquire public funds and serve the larger community.

11. Professionals' classic commitment not to take undue advantage of vulnerable clients is highlighted in how the professional treats elderly people in negotiating their bequests and endowments.

Case analysis teaches that ethics is based on values and derives from interpersonal relationships; ethical dilemmas emerge from conflicting values, and can be resolved through a deliberate process of decision-making. In Jewish communal service, relationships between any parts of the social structure—professionals, lay leaders, clients, agency, community—can create conflicts of ethics. The conflicts can involve non-Jewish staff as well as Jewish staff.

The particularity of ethical dilemmas in Jewish communal service is due to the interaction of the agency's sectarian ideology with the ideology of social work and other professions. Sectarian ideology stems from religion, and professional ideology stems from secular society. The richness of the ethical dilemmas is due to the interface between Jewish values and secular values. When agencies subscribe to both sets of values, they are faced with real conflict that is not easily resolvable. The resolution represents an intellectual and emotional challenge.

PROBLEMS

Professionals in Jewish communal service need time to deliberate over value conflicts and ethical dilemmas before arriving at a resolution. They need to be sensitive to the ethical dimension in their work. In these troubling and pressured times when agencies struggle to survive fiscally, ethics usually occupies a lower rung in their priorities. Perhaps these are some of the reasons why no systematic study of ethics has ever been undertaken in Jewish communal service.

Ethics is the *kol d'mamah dakah* ("still small voice") in the conscience of professionals. It calls when no one is watching or listening, in the privacy of one's thoughts, at home, on the road, or at the office. The individual wrestles with the implications of a choice of actions, and eventually makes a decision. There did not seem to be a need to publicize the process until now. The time has arrived to stimulate professionals to openly share their thoughts and values in order to arrive at sound ethical decisions.

PROSPECTS

Individual practitioners are not the only ones who can benefit from a study of ethics. Agencies are beginning to contemplate the establishment of ethics committees to handle the ethical dilemmas that arise in practice. These usually consist of department heads, led by a staff member who is knowledgeable in the subject and conducts in-service training.

Ethical dilemmas loom larger in times of fiscal crisis. In addition, as the organized Jewish community turns inward and increases its emphasis on Jewish continuity, the agency's sectarian ideology will gain prominence in interaction with professional ideology, thus exacerbating potential value conflicts.

Jews have a long history of ethical deliberation. Pirke Avot (*Eth-*

ics of the Fathers) serves as Judaism's ethical foundation in the social life of the community. With Pirke Avot as their historical context, Jewish communal agencies apply Jewish and professional values and ethics to serving the Jewish and general community in the finest tradition of *tzedakah* (social justice) and *hesed* (loving-kindness).

References

Abramson, M. 1985. The autonomy-paternalism dilemma in social work practice. *Social Casework* 66:7, 385–393.

———. 1989. Autonomy vs. paternalistic beneficence: Practice strategies. *Social Casework* 66, 101–105.

Association of Jewish Center Professionals. 1984. *Code of Ethics.*

Barry, V. 1982. *Moral Aspects of Health Care.* Belmont, Calif.: Wadsworth.

Batshaw, M. 1961. Jewish values in the operation of Jewish communal institutions. Small Cities Conference.

Beauchamp, T., and Childress, J. 1989. 3rd ed. *Principles of Biomedical Ethics.* New York: Oxford.

——— and ———. 1994. 4th ed. *Principles of Biomedical Ethics.* New York: Oxford.

Berger, P. L. 1967. *The Sacred Canopy.* New York: Doubleday.

Binkly, L. 1961. *Contemporary Ethical Theories.* New York: Philosophical Library.

Bleich, J. D. 1981. *Judaism and Healing: Halakhic Perspectives.* New York: Ktav.

——— and Rosner, F., eds. 1979. *Jewish Bioethics.* New York: Sanhedrin Press.

Brandt, R. B. 1983. The real and alleged problems of utilitarianism. *Hastings Center Report* 13:2, 37–43.

Bubis, G. B.; Phillips, B. A.;, Reitman, S. A.; and Rotto, G. S. 1985. The consumer reports: Hiring of entry-level Jewish communal workers. *Journal of Jewish Communal Service* 62:2, 103–110.

Burns, C. R. 1987. A priest's painful choice. *Newsweek*. Feb. 2.

Callahan, D. T. 1984. Autonomy: A moral good, not a moral obsession. *Hastings Report* 14:5, 40–42.

———. 1985. What do children owe elderly parents? *Hastings Center Report* 15:2, 32–37.

Caplan, A. L. 1986. Professional ethics: Virtue or vice. *Jewish Social Work Forum* 2, 1–14.

Chachkes, E. 1988. Ethics in hospital care. *Jewish Social Work Forum* 24, 30–35.

Chanover, H. 1986. Seventy-five years later: Issues confronting central agencies for Jewish education. *Journal of Jewish Communal Service* 63:1, 21–29.

Chazan, B. 1987. A Jewish educational philosophy for Jewish community centers. *Journal of Jewish Communal Service* 63:3, 227–236.

——— and Charendoff, M. 1994. *Jewish Education and the Jewish Community Center*. Israel: Jewish Community Centers Association.

Childress, J. F. 1981. *Priorities in Biomedical Ethics* Philadelphia: Westminster Press.

Conference of Jewish Communal Service. 1984. *Model Code of Ethics*.

Council of Jewish Federations. 1991*a*. *Distribution of Scarce Resources*. 2 vols. New York.

———. 1991*b*. *National Jewish Population Survey*. New York.

Crohn, J. n.d. *Ethnic Identity and Marital Conflict: Jews, Italians, and WASPS*. New York: American Jewish Committee.

Danzig, R. A. 1986. Religious values vs. professional values: Dichotomy or dialectic? *Jewish Social Work Forum* 22:22, 41–53.

Dubin, D. 1986. On Jewish renaissance: Reflections and renewal. *Journal of Jewish Communal Service* 63:1, 33–39.

Etzioni, A. 1991. A new community of thinkers, both liberal & conservative. *Wall Street Journal.* Oct. 8, p. 22.

Feldman, D. 1968. *Birth Control in Jewish Law.* New York: New York University Press.

Feuerman, C. 1983. Critical challenges facing the Jewish day school in the coming decade. *Jewish Education* 20–22.

Freedberg, S. 1989. Self–determination: Historical perspectives and effects on current practice. *Social Work* 34:1, 33–38.

Freundel, B., and Tucker, G. 1993. Homosexuality and halakhic Judaism. *Moment* 18:2.

Germain, C. 1991. *Human Behavior in the Social Environment: An Ecological View* New York: Columbia University Press.

Glaser, B., and Strauss, A. 1967. *The Discovery of Grounded Theory.* New York: Aldine.

Goldman, A. 1980. *The Moral Foundations of Professional Ethics.* Totowa, N.J.: Roman & Littlefield.

Gordon, M. M. 1964. *Assimilation in American Life.* New York: Oxford.

Gordon, W. E. 1962. A critique of the working definition. *Social Work* 7:4, 3–13.

———. 1965. Knowledge and value: Their distinct relationship in clarifying social work practice. *Social Work* 10, 332–39.

Grad, E. 1978. Issues of quality in Jewish education: A critical focus. *Jewish Education* 46:3, 10–15.

Greenberg, I. 1986. Toward a principled pluralism. In *Perspectives.* New York: National Jewish Center for Learning and Leadership.

Grunfeld, I. 1956 *The Sabbath.* London: Sabbath League of Great Britain.

Hastings Center. 1986. AIDS: Public health and civil liberties.

Hastings Center Report 16, 1–36.

Heschel, A. J. *The Sabbath*. 1951. New York: Farrar, Straus & Young.

Howard, R. 1992. Vive la difference! *Baltimore Jewish Times*. Mar. 6.

———; Lipsitz, G.; Sheppard, F.; and Steinitz, L. 1991. An ethics dilemma: Sexual behavior in group residences. *Families in Society* 72, 360–365.

Huberman, S. 1985. Understanding synagogue affiliation. *Journal of Jewish Communal Service* 61:4, 295–304.

Jakobovits, Immanuel. 1972. "Homosexuality." *Encyclopaedia Judaica*. Jerusalem: Keter. 8:962.

Jacobs, L. 1969. *Jewish Ethics, Philosophy and Mysticism*. New York: Behrman House.

Janowsky, O. I. 1948. *The JWB Survey*. New York: Dial Press

Jewish Community Centers Association. 1995. *Task Force on Reinforcing the Effectiveness of Jewish Education in JCCs*. New York.

Jewish Family Service. 1991. *Defining the "J" in JFS*. Baltimore.

Jewish Week. Nov. 5, 1993

Judaism and homosexuality. 1973. *CCAR Journal*. Summer, 31–50.

Johnson, O. A. 1965. *Ethics*. 2nd ed. New York: Holt, Rinehart & Winston.

———. 1984. *Ethics*. 5th ed. New York: Holt, Rinehart & Winston.

Kellner, M. 1978. *Contemporary Jewish Ethics*. New York: Sanhedrin Press.

Lamm, N. 1974. Judaism and the modern attitude to homosexuality. *Encyclopaedia Judaica Yearbook*. Jerusalem: Keter.

Levine, E. 1987. Democracy, pluralism, and American Jewry. Plan of Study. New York: Wurzweiler School of Social Work, Yeshiva University.

Levy, C. S. 1972. Values and planned change. *Social Casework* 53:8, 488–493.

———. 1973. The value base of social work. *Journal of Education for Social Work* 9:4, 34–42.

———. 1974*a*. Advocacy and injustice or justice. *Social Service Review* 48:1, 39–50.

———. 1974*b*. The relevance or irrelevance of consequences to social work ethics. *Journal of Jewish Communal Service* 51:1, 73–81.

———. 1976*a*. *Social Work Ethics*. New York: Human Sciences Press.

———. 1976*b*. Personal versus professional values: The practitioner's dilemma. *Clinical Social Work Journal* 4:2, 110–120.

———. 1976*c*. Social work and the Jewish community center. *Journal of Jewish Communal Service* 53:1, 44–51.

———. 1979. *Values and Ethics for Social Work Practice*. Silver Spring, Md.: National Association of Social Workers.

———. 1982. *Guide to Ethical Decisions and Actions for Social Service Administrators*. New York: Haworth.

———. 1993. *Social Work Ethics on the Line*. New York: Haworth.

Lewis, H. 1984. Ethical assessment. *Social Casework* 203–211.

———. 1986. Response. *Jewish Social Work Forum* 22.

Linzer, N. 1963. Should the Jewish community center be open on the Sabbath? *Jewish Social Work Forum* 1.

———. 1964. The contribution of social work to Jewish survival. *Journal of Jewish Communal Service* 40:3, 316–327.

———. 1978. *The Nature of Man in Judaism and Social Work*. New York: Federation of Jewish Philanthropies.

———. 1986*a*. The obligations of adult children to aged parents: A view from Jewish tradition. *Journal of Aging and Judaism* 1:1, 34–48.

———. 1986*b*. Resolving ethical dilemmas in Jewish communal service. *Journal of Jewish Communal Service* 63:2, 105–117.

————. 1989. Ethical decision-making: Implications for practice. *Journal of Jewish Communal Service* 65, 182–189.

————. 1990. Talmudic and ethical approaches to Soviet Jewish resettlement. *Journal of Jewish Communal Service* 67:2, 118–123.

———— and Lowenstein, L. 1987. Autonomy and paternalism in work with the frail Jewish elderly. *Journal of Aging and Judaism* 2:1 19–34.

Loewenberg, F. M. 1988. *Religion and Social Work Practice in Contemporary American Society.* New York: Columbia University Press.

———— and Dolgoff, R. 1992. *Ethical Decisions for Social Work Practice.* 4th ed. Itasca, Ill.: Peacock.

Maximizing Jewish Educational Effectiveness of Jewish Community Centers. 1984. New York: Jewish Welfare Board.

Mayer, E., and Sheingold, C. 1979. *Intermarriage and the Jewish Future.* New York: American Jewish Committee.

Medding, P. Y.; Tobin, G. A.; Fishman, S. B.; and Rimor, M. 1992. *Jewish Identity in Conversionary and Mixed Marriages.* New York: American Jewish Committee.

Millgram, A. E. 1965. *Sabbath: Day of Delight.* Philadelphia: Jewish Publication Society.

Monson, R. G., and Feldman, R. P. 1991–92. The cost of living Jewishly in Philadelphia. *Journal of Jewish Communal Service* 68:2, 148–159.

National Association of Social Workers. 1967. *Values in Social Work: A Re-Examination.* Silver Spring, Md.

————. 1980. *Code of Ethics.* Silver Spring, Md.

National Jewish Center for Learning and Leadership. 1986. *Perspective.* New York

Neuborne, B. 1987. A flaw in his outlook. *New York Times.* Oct. 4.

Nulman, E. 1984. The morality of social work ethics: A philosophical inquiry. D.S.W. diss. Wurzweiler School of Social Work,

Yeshiva University.

Perlman, H. H. 1976. Believing and doing: Values in social work education. *Social Casework* 57:6, 381–390.

Pritchard, H. A. 1912. Does moral philosophy rest on a mistake? *Mind* 21.

Proctor, E. K.; Morrow-Howell, N.; and Lott, C. L. 1993. Classification and correlates of ethical dilemmas in hospital social work. *Social Work* 38:2, 166–178.

Pumphrey, M. W. 1959. *The Teaching of Values and Ethics in Social Work Education.* Vol. 13 of the Curriculum Study. New York: Council of Social Work Education.

Rabbinical Assembly. 1991. *Proceedings.*

Rabbinical Assembly. 1992. Committee on Jewish Law and Standards.

Rawls, J. 1981. *A Theory of Justice.* Cambridge, Mass: Harvard University Press.

Reamer, F. G. 1982a. *Ethical Dilemmas in Social Service.* New York: Columbia.

———. 1982b. Conflicts of professional duty in social work. *Social Casework* 63,10, 579–585.

———. 1983a. The concept of paternalism in social work. *Social Service Review* 57:2, 254–271.

———. 1983b. Ethical dilemmas in social work practice. *Social Work,* 28:1, 31–36.

Ribner, D. 1991–92. Doing with less: The ethics of diminished resources. *Journal of Jewish Communal Service* 68:2, 192–7.

Ribner, S. 1978. The effects of intensive Jewish education on adult Jewish life-styles. *Jewish Education* 46.

Rokeach, M. 1973. *The Nature of Human Values.* New York: Free Press.

Rosen, B. T. 1985. The role of the Jewish community center and Jewish continuity. *Journal of Jewish Communal Service* 62:2, 118–

128.

Ross, W. D. 1930. *The Right and the Good*. New York: Oxford.

Schiff, A., and Schneider, M. 1994. *The Jewishness Quotient of Jewish Day School Graduates*. Research Report I. New York: David Azrieli Graduate Institute of Jewish Education and Administration, Yeshiva University.

Schiff, A., and Schneider, M. 1994. *Far-Reaching Effects of Extensive Jewish Day School Attendance*. Research Report II. New York: David Azrieli Graduate Institute of Jewish Education and Administration, Yeshiva University.

Schiff, G. 1986. Funding by federation and non-federation sources for Jewish education. *Jewish Education* 54:2, 31–37.

Schindler, A. M. 1986. Will there be one Jewish people in the year 2000? In *Proceedings of a Conference*. New York: National Jewish Center for Learning and Leadership.

Schwartzbaum, A. 1988. *The Bamboo Cradle*. New York: Feldheim.

Siegel, S. 1971. Ethics and the halakhah. *Conservative Judaism* 25.

Silver, D. J., ed. 1970. *Judaism and Ethics*. New York: Ktav.

Siporin, M. 1975. *Introduction to Social Work Practice*. New York: Macmillan.

Sklare, M. 1971. *America's Jews*. New York: Random House.

Solender, Sanford. 1962. The vital future of the Jewish community center in America. *Journal of Jewish Communal Service* 39:1, 42–54.

Solender, Steven. 1983. The federation role in Jewish education. *Jewish Education* 17–19.

Solomon, J. 1994. Ethical Ten Commandments. *Sh'ma* 1.

Soloveitchik, J. B. 1983. *Halakhic Man*. Philadelphia: Jewish Publication Society.

Spots, L. H. 1979. Funding relationships between bureaus and federations. *Jewish Education* 47:1, 14–23.

Toulmin, S. 1981. The tyranny of principles. *Hastings Report* 11:6, 31–39.

UJA-Federation of New York. 1993. "Report of the strategic planning committee." New York.

Wurzburger, W. S. 1978. The need for more balance in Jewish education. *Jewish Education* 46:3, 26–29.

———. 1984. Obligations toward aged parents. *The Jewish Woman in the Middle*. New York: Hadassah.

———. 1994. *Ethics of Responsibility: Pluralistic Approaches to Covenantal Ethics*. Philadelphia: Jewish Publication Society.

Index

of strangers 76–7, 113
principles 17–21, 97, 100, 104
principles screen 51
professional 12–16
seminar 142
sources of 14–17
Ten Commandments 28
theory 17–18, 77–81, 92
Etzioni, A. 21

Federations 68, 73–5, 80, 83–95, 97–104, 113–4, 123, 125, 141, 150, 157, 166–9
Feuerman, C. 156
Fidelity 57, 92, 146, 162,
Freundel, B. 130
Fundraising 83–94, 132–3, 171

Gay couples 132
General ethics 12–14
Germain, C. 6
Goldman, A. 12
Gordon, M. xiii
Gordon, W.E. 4
Grad, E. 155, 161
Greenberg, I. 27
Grunfeld, I. 120

Hachnassat orchim 109
Halakhah 10, 13, 24–6, 124, 129, 172
Heschel, A.J. 120
Hesed 5, 109, 114, 174
Holocaust 24
Homosexuality 10, 29, 128–32
Howard, R. 33, 36, 39, 41–2
Huberman, S. 150

Ideology 29, 107–9, 123, 157, 172
Intermarriage 7, 141–4, 157, 169, 172
Israel 27, 83–5, 93, 95, 98–101, 103–4, 110

Jacobs, L. 23
Jakobovits, I. 130

Janowsky, O. 116–7
Jewish civil religion 27
Jewish communal professionals 12
Jewish communal service 27–30, 42, 171–2
Jewish community 6, 9, 21, 27, 36–43, 46, 71–2, 80, 89. 108–110, 114, 123, 143, 145–7, 148, 151, 160, 171, 173
Jewish Community Center 67, 115–34, 151, 153, 168
Jewish Community Centers Association 117, 134
Jewish continuity 29, 147, 151, 154, 168, 173
Jews from the former Soviet Union 7, 105–114
Jewish education 62, 65, 155–70
Jewish ethics 3, 23–6, 29
Jewish family 9, 12, 71, 151
Jewish Family Service 33, 36–42, 44–52, 67, 135, 141–2, 145, 149–50, 153
Jewish identity 6, 9, 141–5, 151, 156, 158–9, 166, 169
Jewish law 23–6. *See* Halakhah
Johnson, O.A. 14–15

Kant, I. 14
Kashruth 124, 126, 164, 172
Kellner, M. 24

Lamm, N. 128
Levine, E. 26
Levy, C.S. 4, 7, 8, 11–12, 16, 33, 53, 59, 76, 78, 108–9, 116, 162
Lewis, H. 13, 16, 48, 51, 90, 160
Linzer, N. 13, 15, 19, 62, 66, 109, 116, 122
Loewenberg, F. 4, 8, 12, 51, 53, 137
Lowenstein, L. 19

Maimonides, M. 69, 110, 121
Mayer, E. 150, 158
Medding, P. 153
Mill, J.S. 15